The Blessed Mother's Blue Rose of the Healing Heart

7th Edition—Revised with 48 Additional Pages of Profound Teachings

What Readers Say

"The Blessed Mother's Blue Rose of the Healing Heart is a profound book to experience. The gentle beauty of the words creates a space to grow."

Georgia Shakti-Hill, talk show host and author of *Sharing the Light*

"In this beautiful book, Mother Mary's Messenger adds new dimension to Her Message. Thank you, Mary-Ma, for embodying and communicating these powerful messages of comfort and healing."

Kiara Windrider, author of *Doorway to Eternity; A Guide to Planetary Ascension*

"In this book Mother Mary lovingly bestows practices for opening the heart and ascending—ourselves, planet Earth and all beings. The energies created by performing these profound yet simple practices ensure our Ascension."

Juno Dawson, Editor and Heartsong Sound Healer

"The pictures, the prayers, and the teachings — all are encoded with the Light that we need for healing and transformation."

Mikaelah Cordeo, Ph.D., Ascended Master channel and author of *Love Will Steer the Stars*

"I felt a very strong presence when I opened the book. Every page I opened to and every passage I read at random sent chills straight into my heart area."

Rachaell Saan-Ma,
performer of sacred music and dance

" . . . provides the tools to anchor and teach the ascension. . . . This book is a guide to stay focused on the Path of the Heart."

Sakkara Heartsong, founder of The Hathor Temple of Light and Sound Mystery School

"A woman in our prayer group told us that her grandson was in a hospital in a near death state.

"When I arrived home that night, I realized I had taken on the sorrow and the tragedy of these people. I felt overcome with emotion. My heart felt full of sorrow, and I overflowed with tears.

"When my husband got home, he sat with me. We prayed *The Rosary of Tribulation Prayer*. Instantly, the overwhelming emotions I had taken on were transmuted, and I felt totally released and clear."

Jane McClung

I've been waiting for seven years to find something like this."

Lynn Butler, Blue Rose World Service Group leader

"It gave me total clarity of why I am here! It resounded in my soul."

Danali Jordon, spiritual teacher, Share the Wisdom Publishing Company"

"I so much appreciate *The Blessed Mother's Blue Rose of the Healing Heart*. I have been saying *The Blessed Ascension Rosary*, and I can feel and see the positive changes that have occurred in my family."

Martiena Bartholemew

"Spirit nudged me to buy this book. I resisted all day. . . . I read it on the airplane on the way home and found it fascinating; it contained Truths and insights I had never before heard. Reading it felt like a revelation and initiation at times, while some of it spoke straight to my heart."

Birgit Smother

"Of all the Mother Mary books and transmissions that I have read, I highly recommend this one."

Kuthumi John

"What a book! What wonderous writings"

Rita Peterson

"I am comforted by this book and the prayers."

Janay DeRyke, twenty-year old seeker

Book Review

by Tiziana Della Rovere

Mother Mary's desire is to awaken our hearts to Her Presence. This inspired book draws us closer to Her, offering a cornucopia of information, guidance, and practices that will bring delight to those who are devoted to the Beloved Mother.

The book is organized in two parts—the Outer Mysteries and the Inner Mysteries. The Outer Mysteries contains innovative prayers, teachings about the ascension process, and guidelines on how to set up devotional groups in your community. It also includes extensive information about the history and symbology of the Rosary which focuses on the Resurrected Christ and de-emphasizes the Crucifixion aspect.

In the Inner Mysteries, the Lineage of the Grail, Mary Magdalene and the Black Madonna are introduced as Mysterious Truths for us to meditate upon as a reflection of the journey which is both personal and universal.

The Blessed Mother's Blue Rose of the Healing Heart is a Grace-filled tribute of Love from Mary Clarice McChrist, the result of her lifelong dedication to the service of Mother Mary.

Tiziana Della Rovere is author of the books: *The Sacred Fire and Adorata—Recovering the Feminine Soul* and her sacred art companion cards *Mother Mary's Little Flowers of the Soul—A Practical Guide to Our Devotional Life.*

The Blessed Mother's Blue Rose of the Healing Heart

Mary Clarice McChrist

Messenger for

Lord Mary
Cosmic Mother of the Christos

Lotus-Rose Publications
Mount Shasta, California

The Blessed Mother's Blue Rose of the Healing Heart
7th Edition — Revised with 48 Additional Pages of Profound Teachings

Formerly published by the Mother Matrix as:
The Novena for the Healing Heart

Copyright © 2003 by Mary Clarice McChrist

All rights reserved. No part of this book may be reproduced, transmitted or utilized in any form or by any means, electronic, photographic, mechanical (including photocopy) recordings, or any information, storage, or retrieval system without written permission from the publisher, except for brief quotations embodied in literary articles or reviews or the sharing of *The Blessed Ascension Rosary Prayer*.

For permissions, condensations, translations or adaptations, write the publisher at the address below.

Ascension / Channeling / Mysticism
ISBN 0-9710677-8-3

First edition: 1992
Second edition: 1993
Third edition: 1996
Fourth revised edition: 1997
Fifth revised edition: 1999
Sixth revised and enlarged edition: 2001
Seventh revised and enlarged edition: 2003

Mary Clarice McChrist may be contacted at:
The Mother Matrix
Post Office Box 1178
Mount Shasta, California 96067

Toll Free Phone: 866-223-0597; or (530) 235-4117
Web Site: mother-matrix.org   E-mail: mary-ma@mother-matrix.org

Published by:
Lotus-Rose Publications
P. O. Box 1178
Mt. Shasta, California 96067

Printed in the United States of America

The Virgin of Adoration
by Fra Filippo Lippi

Gifts of Mary

"I come in this intense time of transition
to reveal My Gifts to all beings
who call upon the Name of the Mother.
Therefore, beloved ones, I present this
precious volume, that you and yours,
that the Entire Body of the Christ,
might be released and freed by your own
atonement (at-One-ment) with Source."

The Blessed Mother,
Lord Mary

Dedication

To Mother Mary for Her Eternal Inspiration, Love, and Divine Grace.

To my dear Master, El Morya Khan, who placed me firmly upon the Path.

To Jesus, my brother and teacher, who silently guided my actions.

To you, the brave souls who have descended to Earth from the far reaches of Creation in order to discover that You are God.

To my parents who taught me how to Love.

To my children who taught me what motherhood was and was not.

To my grandchildren who ignited in me the Joy of the Mother.

To Opal, age four, who freed my inner child and taught me how to sing again.

Table of Contents

Gifts of Mary v
Dedications vi
Illustrations xiv
Appreciation xvi
Introduction to the Book xvii

Book One: The Outer Mysteries

Introduction to the Outer Mysteries 3

Chapter 1 - Our Lady Lord Mary

Heart of Mary 7
Lord Mary's Letter 11-20-93 8
Lord Mary's Letter 8-10-97 11
Mother Mary's Sacrifice for Humanity 14
Mary's Name Change 16
The Mother Matrix 19

Chapter 2 - Mary's Sacred Gardens

The Grotto of Our Lady of the Roses 22
Our Lady of All Nations Garden 24
A Plea to All Nations in 2000 28

Chapter 3 - The Blessed Ascension Rosary

What is the Rosary? 33
History of the Rosary 33
The Blessed Ascension Rosary 35
Symbolism of the Rosary 36
Your Flame of God Individuality 38

Effect of Reciting the Blessed Ascension Rosary ... 39
Claiming Your Ascension Now!.............................. 42

Chapter 4 - The Ascension Process

My Easter Message: Focus on Ascension 45
What is Ascension? 46
What is Service? 47
Ascension as a Group Project 47
I Am the Way 50
The Ascension Process 51
Defining Ascension 51
Have You Ascended? 53
Service and Ascension 56
Your Personal Mission 56
The Inner Plane Ascension Ritual 57

Chapter 5 - World Service Devotions

Mary Speaks on the Power of Prayer 60
Mary Speaks on Your Daily Ritual 62
Mary Speaks on Faith 63
Prayer of Unified Faith 64
World Service Prayer 66
My Family Prayer 67
Divine Mercy for Our Ancestors 68
Lord Michael 70
Tube of Light 72
Auric Safety Decree 74
Personal Protection from Archangel Michael 75
Invocation for Ascension 76
Ascension Fire Decree 78

Chapter 6 - Blue Rose Prayers

Rosary Instructions 80
Blue Rose Prayers 82
   1. Attunement to Mary 82
   2. Mary Is with You 82
   3. Message from Saint Germain 84
   4. Lord Mary's Promise to Her Children 85
   5. Prologue for Blue Rose 86
   6. Matrix of the Mother 87
   7. A World Dispensation 88
      Protection and Purity 89
   8. Your Rosary Beads 91
   9. Rosary of Tribulation 92
   10. Our Mother's Prayer 94
   11. O Dove of Peace 95
   12. The Lord's Prayer 96
   12. The New Lord's Prayer 96
   13. AUM - All United in Mary 97
   14. Mary's Communion Prayer 98
   15. The Blessed Ascension Rosary 99
   16. Lord Mary's Call 100
   17. The Blessed Ascension Rosary 101
   18. The Prayer for the Beloved Children 103
   19. The Rosary for the Inner Child 104
   20. The Transmutation of World Sorrow 107
   21. The Black Madonna Rosary 109
   22. The Immaculate Concept Prayer 110
   23. The Ascension Rosary - Conclusion 112

24. I Am Your Mother 113
25. Increasing the Rosary Momentum 114
26. Sign of the Cross 115
27. Closing Prayer 116
28. Cosmic Mother's Sealing Prayer 118
29. Ave Maria 119
30. I Am Presence Song..................................... 120
30. Transmission from Mother Mary 121
31. Lord Mary's Request................................... 121
32. Mary's Rose Crusade for World Peace....122

Chapter 7 - Blue Rose World Service Groups

The Purpose of the Blue Rose Groups 124
Blue Rose World Service Groups 125
My Ambassadors of Peace 126
Creating Your Blue Rose Event 128
Preparing the Sanctuary 128
Aligning Your Home 129
Anchoring the Violet Flame 129
Calling Forth the Cities of Light 130
The Altar Focus 132
Dedication for Blue Rose World Service Work 133
Anchoring the Light 133
The Power of Music 134
The Double Dorje 134
Blue Rose World Service Group Format 136
Grounding the Energy and Intention 138
Group Leaders... 139
Group Initiation 141
What Is a Messenger?... 141
Discrimination - Testing the Spirit 143

Chapter 8 - Winning the Protection Game

Winning the Protection Game 148
Archangel Michael 148
The Sword of Michael 149
Archangel Michael Speaks 150
The Noble Sword of Michael 150
Using Your Sword of Truth 151
Are You Corded? 152
My Sovereignty Prayer 154
The Rainbow Protection of Archangel Michael ... 156
Accept Your Divine Authority 158
Total Cosmic Christ Protection 159

Book Two: The Inner Mysteries

Introduction to the Inner Mysteries 162
My Lady's Quest 165

Chapter 1 - The Holy Grail

The Holy Grail - A Legacy to Cherish 168
The Lineage of the Holy Grail 169
The Secret Order of the Blue Rose 170

Chapter 2 - White Madonna Black Madonna

The White Madonna 174
Mary's Early Temple Training 174
Mary the Lioness 175
The Black Madonna - Lady of Mystery 178
Jesus and the Magdalene 178
Jesus Speaks to His Beloved 180
The Miracle of the Thorn Tree 182

Chapter 3 - What is Embodiment?

Embodiment of the Christ 184
Embodiment of the Divine Mother 186
What Will You Embody? 187

Chapter 4 - The Flaming Hearts

Flaming Hearts of Mary and Jesus 192
Becoming the Flaming Heart - Practice 193
Preparing Your Heart 194
The Golden Heart Door 194
Ceremony of Healing and Initiation 196
    Blue Flame 198
    Gold Flame 199
    Purple Flame 199
    Pink Flame 200
    Raspberry Flame 201
    Silver Flame 201
    Again, Raspberry 202
    Meditation with Flames 202
    Green Flame 203

Chapter 5 - The Secret Mysteries

The Six Secret Mysteries 208
    The Mystery of Giving 211
    The Mystery of Forgiving 212
    The Mystery of Multiplying 213
    The Mystery of the Black Madonna 215
    The Mystery of the White Madonna 217
    The Mystery of the One 218

Homage to the White Madonna	219
Appendix of Sacred Music	221
Music to Our Lady	222
The Mother/Goddess	223
Lovely Music	223
A Powerful Experience	224
Mother Mary Teaching	224
Glossary of Divine Beings	225
Supreme Mother	231
Glossary of Terms	232
The Mother Matrix Web Site	240
Spiritual Evaluations	241
The Blessed Mother's Blue Rose of the Healing Heart with Optional CD	242
Mother Matrix Order Form	243
Visionary Art, Cards, and Photos	244
About the Author	245

Illustrations

Madonna of the Blue Rose .... Cover
   by Unknown Artist

Mary Clarice McChrist ....Back Cover
   Photograph by Diane Hollcraft

The Virgin in Adoration iv
   by Fra Filippo Lippi

Madonna of the Blue Rose 2
   by Unknown Artist

The Immaculate Heart of Mary 6
   by Unknown Artist from House of David

Mary Blessing the Earth 14
   by Unknown Artist

The Lord Mary Triptych 18
   by Mary Sylvia McChrist

Grotto of Our Lady of the Roses 23
   Photograph by Mary Sylvia McChrist

Goddess Quan Yin Gazebo 24
   Photograph by Diana Hollcraft

Our Lady of All Nations Peace Garden 27
   Photograph by Diana Hollcraft

Mary of the Diamond Heart 32
   by Mary Sylvia McChrist

Diagram of Rosary Beads 37

Cosmic Eight 40

Lord Jesus - The Shroud of Turin 44
   Photograph Touched by Sai Baba

Mary with Rosary - 79
   Apparition - Scottsdale - Photographer Unknown

Mary in Italy 90
   Apparition - Photographer Unknown

Madonna of the Streets 102
   by Roberto Ferrussi

Our Lady of the Rose 105
   by Enrico Reffo, Turin

The Black Madonna 106
   by Mary Sylvia McChrist

The Black Madonna /Mary Magdalene 108
   Apparition - Photographer Unknown

Lord Mary Buddha 111
   by Mary Sylvia McChrist

Madonna and Child 117
   by William Adolph Bougereau 1825-1905

Double Dorje 135

Apparition Photograph of Lord Michael 146
   Photographer Unknown

Inner Mysteries 160
   Woodcut - 18th Centurt - Artist Unknown

I Serve the Grail 166
   by Mary Sylvia McChrist

Mary of the Flaming Heart 190
   Woodcut -18th Century - Artist Unknown

The Accolade 206
   by E. B. Leighton - 19th Century England

Appreciation

Mother Mary thank you for this long Heart journey of birthing your precious Blue Rose Book.

Jesus Christ, my overwhelming gratitude to You for overseeing my life and sharing so many of Your Inner Mysteries with me. Now You have given permission to release this work to your children.

Archangel Michael, Your Protection and Initiation brought safety and Peace—thank you.

Saint Padre Pio, my editor in Spirit, bless your accuracy and the discipline of your gentle focus. I Am deeply touched that you have chosen to work on this project.

Much Love to Juno Dawson, my new sister in Light, who lovingly edited this book on the physical plane.

My deep appreciation to Jonathan Lake who was instrumental in the data entry work of both the sixth and seventh editions. His encouragement, dedication, and commitment to the task have been remarkable.

Special thanks to Aaron and Bonnie at Heaven on Earth Project. Aaron answered a million computer and publishing questions and brought the cover sketch to its final perfection. God bless you both.

Jane and Robert McClung, Our beloved Angels, contributed to this wonderful cause by allowing the Beloved Mother Mary's Blue Rose Book to reach Her children. *Without funding, the publication process would have been impossible to complete. Both Mary and I are eternally grateful for their generosity. May the Great Mother bless and keep them always in Her Flaming Heart.*

Introduction to the Book

I awoke feeling the dazzling Presence of Mother Mary. The room was full of Light.

"Women are freed from the Curse of Eve," She stated calmly. I burst into tears as the emotion of Her words hit me.

"Take your pen, paper, and write." Mother Mary began dictating to me. *The Keys to the Golden Age* was the product of the messages She gave me.

Since then, 1976, Mother Mary has become one of my dearest friends. She consoles, nurtures, teaches, heals, and has prepared me to bring forth *The Blessed Mother's Blue Rose of the Healing Heart* for you to also know Her Love and Her Grace.

Mother Mary offers: *The Blessed Ascension Rosary* is my most profound prayer for this age. Why? Because daily recitation of this prayer allows you to win your ascension over the third and fourth dimensional world. Moving beyond duality, you begin to create Heaven on Earth."

Our Lady also asks you to prayer *The Rosary of Tribulation*, which specifically addresses and heals all issues facing humankind.

Mother Mary may inspire you to create a Blue Rose World Service Group. She explains exactly how to do this: to prepare your sanctuary and altar; anchor in the Light; and to purify with sage, bells, the Violet Flame of Saint Germain, music, and mantra.

She discusses scheduling, discrimination, the testing of the Spirit, and the Power of Divine Love in creating your group.

Archangel Michael gives a practical guide of tools and techniques for protecting yourself and your loved ones. Michael actually Initiates you and offers His Dispensation of your own Sword of Truth.

Jesus' teachings of Unknown Mysteries include His sacred relationship with the Black Madonna as well as the Twelve Christs. You will also discover Lord Jesus and Mother Mary's connection with Camelot, the Lineage of the Holy Grail, the Mystical Order of the Blue Rose, and the Six Secret Mysteries.

Mary Clarice McChrist
In Service to the Mother and the Christ

Book One

The Outer Mysteries

*Madonna of the Blue Rose
by Unknown Artist of Mexico*

Introduction to the Outer Mysteries

My Dear Children,

I have drawn you to this precious book, *The Blessed Mother's Blue Rose of the Healing Heart*, for it will help direct you through the earthly maze of World Tribulation. This prophesied time of outer earth changes—earthquakes, floods, pestilence, and violence—is being equally mirrored by a disruptive inner transmutation of your ego, personality, and psyche.

All of your past traumas, dramas, and your shadow self, must be cleared and your body purified. Your ancestors and lineage affect your life, your karma, and your personal ascension. Your DNA is altering and increasing from two to twelve strands. *You are becoming a Divine Being in form.*

These prayers are vital for personal and world healing. They will calm and comfort you as you move through profound inner changes. Your Personal Devotion will place you under My Blue Mantle of Divine Grace.

Read Book One. Devour it! Ingest the prayers, and make them part of your being. You will gain My Protection, Power, and Peace.

I Am Lord Mary, Mother of the Cosmic Christ

Chapter 1

Our Lady Lord Mary

*Immaculate Heart of Mary
by Unknown Artist of the House of David*

Heart of Mary

Heart of Mary inflame me,
Soul of Mary open me,
Tears of Mary wash me,
Touch of Mary console me,
Vision of Mary inspire me,
Angels of Mary protect me.

Prayers of Mary uplift me,
Patience of Mary guide me,
Hope of Mary fill me,
Love of Mary expand me,
Charity of Mary see me,
Faith of Mary reassure me.

Guidance of Mary instruct me,
Message of Mary pour through me,
Mercy of Mary heal me,
Surrender of Mary humble me,
Motherhood of Mary express through me,
Godliness of Mary grow in me.

Mother Mary

Mary Clarice McChrist

Lord Mary's Letter   11-20-93

Dear Children,

I Am your beloved Mother. You are My children. I Am Mary, the Mother of all of God's children, regardless of your race, your religion, your culture, or your sex.

When My Son walked the Earth as Christ Jesus, I held for Him His Immaculate Concept. That is, I held in My Heart/Mind His Perfect Blueprint— knowing and seeing His perfection and wholeness as a child of the Mother-Father God. Upon the Ascension of Christ and My Ascension as well, My Work expanded to include all human life on Mother Earth. Now, beloved ones, I hold the Immaculate Concept for each one of you, for truly I Am your Mother.

I manifest Myself in unique ways, wearing radiant garments and appearing under various titles. My basic Message is the same, but I alter My Words according to the beliefs and understandings of the recipients. I come as Mary, Mother of the Christ Child; as Lord Mary, Mother of the Christos; as the Virgin of Guadalupe; or the Rainbow Madonna/Lord Mary Buddha. We are all One, unified as the Mother of all people.

Have you ever wondered why I appear to some visionaries and not to others?

I choose my visionaries for many reasons, some known only to Me and My Son. Most of them are innocents, having a childlike essence and a Purity of

Heart. I know they will receive Me clearly and will not judge or alter My Message. Young children are often chosen because of their pure and honest hearts.

Mary Clarice McChrist (Mary-Ma) is one of My Messengers. Mary-Ma holds the Essence of both Lord Jesus and Myself. She is trained in many traditions and was chosen partly because of her openness. We have worked with her for many lifetimes.

Mary-Ma holds the Sacred Hearts of Lord Mary and Lord Jesus, which We anchored within her Being March 5, 1991. Since then, We have descended and unified Our Essence with her physical form. Supporting Christ's Work, Mary-Ma blends My Mission with that of Lord Jesus. This means Our Missions are One.

Jesus' Mission is now one of Synthesis—bringing together East and West, friend and foe. His Compassion and Wisdom melt old limitations and dogma, which pit one race or religion against another. I also work with humanity to achieve this goal. I come to My children bearing Gifts of Healing, Comfort, and Divine Love.

Hear me, I Am Mary, the Bridge to the Son (Sun). May *The Blessed Mother's Blue Rose of the Healing Heart* lift you to the next level of Wholeness. If some of the vocabulary is unfamiliar to you, refer to the Glossary at the end of this book.

Know that I stand beside you. Keep your hearts

open. Feel My Love and know that you will heal.

I Am Lord Mary come to hold you in My Heart of Purity. I see you as you truly are: whole, perfect, sinless, and worthy. Drop your fetters, the old clothes of the past, and be free!

I Am your Mother; your are My children. Let us create together the time of Peace, Love, and Divine Order according to the Will of God.

I Am Lord Mary,
Mother of the Cosmic Christ
Mary Clarice McChrist

Lord Mary's Letter 8-10-97

Dear Children,

I have come to the Earth again and again at different times, to different countries, incarnating over and over, that you might know Me as your Mother.

You see, I work on the Earth through several bodies—incarnations of Myself. I also work on the etheric, the nonphysical levels of existence, which have no limitations. This enables Me to be everywhere at once, if that is My desire. Like My Son Jesus, Lord Buddha, Saint Francis, all of the Ascended Masters, and yourself, I have a specific Mission in the world.

My mission is to save all life and to lift life into its full radiance and potential. Together, all humanity shall be lifted into the Flame of the Ascension at the closing of this cycle.

Originally, the target date was 2012, but, beloved ones, the date has been moved forward to the year 2008. What does this mean? Will the Earth end and will all life cease? No, beloved ones, life will continue, but duality will be gone forever from the Earth. Oneness will have been achieved. This is My Prophecy of Heaven on Earth.

On the Inner Levels of existence, this is already completed. The matrix or geometric pattern has been engineered and set into place by the Elohim. The Archangels have also played their part in anchoring the quadrants into the Crystalline Grid of the Earth.

All human life is called to assist in two ways. The

first assignment, for those of you who wish to accept it, is to totally renovate your being. *The Blessed Ascension Rosary* will assist you in altering, healing, and transmuting all of your bodies: physical, emotional, mental, and spiritual. As you support Me by healing yourself, My Assistance is directly given to you.

The second form of assistance is to aid in the transformation of Beloved Mother Earth. This Earth requires your world service in the form of sound, light, and color. Prayers, decrees, mantras, music, and songs all transform matter, altering the environment on many levels. Light created as sound is projected outward. Color is frozen sound and light vibrations. All three work in tandem to shift consciousness and matter.

As you uplift your words, speaking your thoughts consciously, your word creations become purified. When your I Am Presence sounds the Sacred Words, your DNA begins to alter. All remaining on Earth will have a 12-strand DNA in full operation by the end of 2003. Many will be God-Realized by 2001 and will have ascended through dimensional levels four and five. Thus you will be ready to receive and hold your Divine Solar Body. Your Divine Diamond Matrix of the Golden Age will be anchored and activated.

My blessings are upon you. Be not afraid. This is a fabulous time to be incarnated upon this planet. Never before has such remarkable repatterning occurred upon a planet. This is a co-creation on all levels.

Congratulations. We are facing the challenge together. Hold with Me the Immaculate Blueprint of God's Victory.

I Am Lord Mary, Your Mother

Mary Clarice McChrist

Mother Mary's Sacrifice for Humanity

*Mary Blessing the Earth
by Unknown Artist*

Some beings pray to the Father, some to the Son, some to the Holy Spirit. Many have forgotten that the Divine Mother is the closest immediate help for all humanity. I, Mary, have chosen to remain totally connected with the emotional body of humanity.

What does this mean? How is this different from most of the Ascended Masters, and God and Goddess Beings of the various religions tradition? Most God-Beings have kept their vibrations far above the Earth's rate of 7-8 cycles per second.

Cosmic Cycles are now raising the Earth's vibration. As consciousness is raised and My children awaken, they must keep pace with these changes. When the vibration reaches 13 cycles per second, the planet will move into the fifth dimension. Then Spirit Beings like Myself will feel more comfortable on Earth.

Meanwhile, because I Love you so much, I have chosen to minister to these lower dimensions in order to be close to you. This is a great sacrifice little understood by My children.

Call upon Me. I Am here for you.

Mother Mary, come forth. (3x)

I Am Lord Mary,
Mother of the Cosmic Christ
Mary Clarice McChrist

Author's note: Often Mother Mary statues or icons shed real tears, sometimes even blood. Why does Mary cry? It is because She truly feels our feelings. She knows our pains. She is attempting to heal our wounds. She truly is our Mother.

I cried for hours when I first integrated into my being Mother Mary's Great Sacrifice for humanity. Most people do not have any understanding of Her Sacrifice.

Mary's Name Change

We are honored to announce
these name changes to the world.

Beloved Mother Mary was honored on December 31, 1991, by the Heavenly Hierarchy. Her Beloved Son, Lord Jesus, the Christ, announced Her new name as "Lord Mary, Cosmic Mother of the Christos".

Lord Jesus, the Christ has likewise assumed an advanced position in the Heavens and He now holds the title of "Cosmic Christ" for this universe.

Lord Mary is the Bridge to the Sun (Son). She connects humanity with Lord Jesus, the Cosmic Christ, and intercedes on our behalf.

Mother of us all, the Blessed Mary comes not just to Catholics, but to people of all races, creeds, colors, and religions. She has appeared countless times around this planet bringing Her Message of Urgency, Hope, and Comfort.

May we open our hearts to receive Her words:

"I offer you My Love eternally.

Give Me the Gift of your Rosary Prayer;
I give you the Gift of My Grace".

Mary asks that you recite *The Blessed Ascension Rosary* daily for yourself and for Mother Earth.

"**No prayer is as effective to My earthly work as the Rosary Prayer.** The energy momentum released in its recitation is multiplied and directed toward personal and planetary healing."

Please join the Beloved Mother in this great group work.

Have you felt Mother Mary's Love? Our Lady's Presence washes us clean with Her Tears of Joyful Compassion. She opens our hearts, renewing our dedication and devotion to healing Mother Earth and Her precious children.

I Am honored to be one of Mary's embodiments and to have established The Mother Matrix to further the work of beloved Lord Mary, Our Mother.

I Am Mary-Ma McChrist,

Standing in the Flame of Mary

in Oneness with your heart

The Lord Mary Triptych
by Mary Sylvia McChrist

The Mother Matrix

The Mother Matrix is a physical plane construct of an eternal Inner Plane focus of the collective Mother. Physically, it is a central focus for the Cosmic Mother.

Inspired by Mother Mary, Mary-Ma McChrist created the shrine in her home in Mount Shasta, California in 1991. This Temple of the Divine Mother was transferred, in 1999, to Mary-Ma's new home in Dunsmuir, California, which is within the radiance of the Sacred Vortex of Mt. Shasta.

Beloved Mary, now advanced to the position of Lord Mary, Mother of the Cosmic Christ, oversees and inspires the activities and creative flow of this center, which remains etherically anchored above Mt. Shasta.

The Mother Matrix is a living focus for Mary's children to gather and experience the Love and Comfort of the Holy Mother.

At this time, *the work of Lord Mary and Lord Jesus Christ is the synthesis of all religions.* People must move beyond their religious prejudices and judgments. All need to honor the Paths of Truth. The Mother Matrix fosters this principle.

A temple room honors Lord Mary and the Divine Mother of many nations and religions. Beloved Mother Tara of Tibet and Lord Mary Buddha, along with Quan Yin, Goddess of Mercy, represent

Buddhism. Beloved Mother Mary is honored in Christianity. Goddess Mothers Gayatri, Lakshmi, and Durga represent Hinduism. White Buffalo Calf Woman embodies the Mother Flame in the Native American teachings. Lord Buddha and Lord Jesus are honored as the Lotus and the Rose. They, along with Lord El Morya, hold the Flame of the Father for the Mother Matrix.

Two very special gardens are connected to the Mother Matrix: The Grotto of Our Lady of the Roses in Mount Shasta, California, and the World Peace Garden next to the Mother Temple in Dunsmuir, California.

Mary Clarice McChrist

Chapter 2

Mary's Sacred Gardens

The Grotto of Our Lady of the Roses

(1992-1997)

The Grotto of Our Lady of the Roses is a sacred space which was created in 1992 by Mary-Ma. This garden is on Alder Street, adjacent to Lake Street, in Mt. Shasta, California. Mother Mary hopes this small wetland will be donated or purchased for Her pilgrims.

This garden project began with the natural beauty of a small grotto, a waterfall, and a stream. Loving hands of Marian devotees created a tiny bridge and a small healing pool lined with sacred rocks, and adorned with candles and roses. Devotees often brought flowers to enhance this natural outdoor temple.

Lord Mary promised to appear in this grotto when the momentum of Light reached an apex of intense desire to see Her. Small miracles and inner visions have already occurred. Several people have seen the Holy Mother. Others report feelings of Peace and Divine Comfort, and have experienced personal healing in this unique space. Mary has spoken telepathically numerous times from the grotto through Mary-Ma and others.

Mother Mary blessed the grotto water for healing on October 15, 1992. The Ascension Flame was anchored in the grotto by Lord Jesus on Easter

Grotto Photograph by Mary Sylvia McChrist

Sunday, 1994. Lord Jesus officially blessed His Mother's Garden as a sanctuary for all people.

More and more healings occurred in the grotto, including a woman who, while reading *The Blessed Mother's Blue Rose of the Healing Heart,* discovered her glasses were still in her purse. She then realized that her eyesight had been corrected. When Lord Mary blessed another woman at the grotto stream through Mary-Ma, the woman received a healing of a seriously fractured wrist and high blood pressure. Her doctor was amazed.

Others have healed their long-held sense of abandonment and separation from the Divine Mother, as well as their sense of abandonment and separation from their human mother. This was a garden of miracles.

Our Lady of All Nations Garden

Come to the Garden of Our Lady of All Nations. It is a place of peace, serenity, and beauty. Mary Clarice McChrist was inspired by Lord Jesus to create this new garden next to her home.

Goddess Quan Yin Gazebo
Photograph by Diana Hollcraft

The Peace Garden is open to the public for meditation and prayer, from 9:00 AM - 9:00 PM. Visitors may simply enter the fenced garden to the right of the driveway. It is located in Dunsmuir, near Mount Shasta, in Northern California. Children must be accompanied by an adult.

This meditation sanctuary was dedicated Easter Sunday, April 23, 2000. This garden features a statue of Mother Mary as Our Lady of All Nations. She oversees a star-tetrahedron matrix of rock with pansies and flowers whose colors represent all of the major races of the Earth. There is a double pond and a triple waterfall symbolizing the Triple Goddess and the Divine Mother's Heart.

A Vesica Piscis Rose Garden anchors the Divine Goddess and was connected directly into the Christ Grid of Earth on May 5, 2000, Grand Alignment Day. The Gazebo of Quan Yin, Goddess of Mercy, was created for private meditation and prayer.

Mother Mary has dedicated this lovely garden sanctuary to World Peace.

"I come with permission of the Father to bring the world a Dispensation of Divine Peace. Tell My children to bring a crystal, a rock, or a small treasure which they are to infuse with prayers for the healing of all nations.

"I call all My children unto Me. Let this be a covenant between Myself as Mother and My beloved sweet children. It is the Mother and Son within each heart and My children who will save the Earth.

"As you place your gift in this garden, also anchor your vision for World Peace. Imagine all children of God living in peace and prosperity. As Divine Mother, I hold this constant vision within My Sacred Heart. Your gift may be placed at the feet of the Mother Mary, Jesus, or Quan Yin statues.

"The purpose of this is to build a powerful prayer momentum within the garden. My garden is open to people of all faiths, religions, races, and creeds. Love offerings for garden maintenance are accepted but never required. Donations of time and plants, as well as volunteer gardeners, are always welcome.

"Please come, your Mother calls you.

"Know I Love the Earth, each nation, each religion, each being, for I Am your Mother."

Our Lady of All Nations

Christ's Personal Blessing

"I wish to personally thank all who have worked on the Peace Garden of Our Lady of All Nations. My blessing on each person, especially those who give this work as a gift. My Grace and the Grace of Mother Mary come upon you now. Many new helpers will come forth to join the others in order to complete and later maintain this garden. I bless each of you."

Lord Jesus, the Cosmic Christ

Mary Clarice McChrist

Our Lady of All Nations Peace Garden
Photograph by Diana Hollcraft

A Plea to All Nations in 2000
by Our Lady of All Nations

O Children of the world, I come forth to you as your loving and patient Mother, Our Lady of All Nations.

I embrace all of the children of this world, synthesizing all nations under the Banner of My Son, Lord Jesus, the Cosmic Christ. *Our Work between 2000 -2005 is to heal the separation and to transmute the bitterness of one nation against the other.*

As your Mother, I draw all nations together, healing the past, opening the hearts of all people, and beseeching you, this planet, these nations, all people, to realize: *Our very survival depends on a common vision and our ability to drop our mistrust and barriers of race and religion. Only as one people united can we survive the hardships facing the Beloved Earth at this time. For this truly is the Tribulation.*

We are One People created from One Source, known and realized in diverse manners and expressed through Avatars—Spiritual World Teachers who took on garments of flesh, physical vehicles, and came forth into various parts of the world. These great Saints and Sages are beyond the time and space of this moment. The Truths they taught express the diversity of the Creator Source. Yet each in their own individual Path created new threads of strength and beauty, adding to the expanding tapestry of human endeavor. All Paths lead to the One Light.

When individuals leave this planet in the experience called death, they transcend their life, their nation, their sex, their creed, and their religion. Though their beliefs are varied, each being is given the awesome opportunity to merge with the Great White Light. This merging erases all else, and the soul goes back into Source.

Today the people of Earth teeter on a precipice of extinction because hearts, minds, souls, and nations are encrusted with judgment, hatred, rebelliousness, and separation.

I stand before you pleading with you, all nations of the world, to stop your battles. *Wake up and know that if you do not come together in LOVE, the planet, all nations, all religions, and all people, will perish.*

I have seen both choices and both results. I have stood many times before the Father God and pleaded on your behalf, on behalf of all people, that this small planet might be allowed the time required to heal its wounds and open to the Heart Light within each human breast.

You are born into this world and you are released from life. You are given free will to alienate yourselves or to come together as ONE HEART.

The heartbeat of humanity calls for Life, for Love, and for Peace. Imagine a world in which a child could be born without the fears of those who walked before, the past generations. Imagine a child who knows only Love, Peace, and Harmony. Envision with me, a child who has food, security, and health, who lives in a World of Peace, knowing all people as his or her extended family.

As Divine Mother of All Nations, I hold this vision firmly within My Sacred Heart.

Move with Me in consciousness; this opportunity has been extended to you by Source. I come with permission of the Father to bring this world a Dispensation of Divine Peace.

Those who are in the United Nations, and those who are spread across this planet, I now challenge all My children: Go into your own hearts, open up, melt with the great cleansing fires which are now released from My Heart to the hearts of all who inhabit this planet. You do not have to believe in Me or agree with what I say within these pages, for this Sacred Dispensation now flows to all My children, and We shall have Our Sweet Reward!

Know I Love the Earth and each nation, each religion, each being.

I Am Your Mother

Mary Clarice McChrist

Chapter 3

The Blessed Ascension Rosary

Mary of the Diamond Heart
by Mary Sylvia McChrist

The Blessed Ascension Rosary

What is the Rosary?

The Rosary is a small prayer which has had a profound impact upon the world. Though it is a mere two stanzas long, the original Rosary Prayer has raised consciousness from the gross perversion which regarded women as solely responsible for the fall of Adam and as a class below man. Today there has been much progress made, for women are protected and treated with dignity throughout many parts of the world.

The role of Mary, of Myself, is to raise the Mother Flame within all beings so that the harmonizing of the Mother-Father within might result in the giving birth to your own Holy Christ Child, the Rose of Sharon. The Gift of the Rosary comes forth, as demanded, by the accumulated Christ Presence of a particular age.

History of the Rosary

In the thirteenth century AD, I, Mary, appeared to Domingo De Gusman, known today as Saint Dominic. He was a sincere disciple who founded the Dominican Order in the year 1203. Because of the darkness of that time, I brought forth the original Rosary through that messenger.

The Rosary has been recited by Catholics for centuries, yet much of its inner meaning has been lost. The Catholic Church has not recently emphasized the use of the Rosary, yet it is of great importance as we move into the Aquarian Age.

In 1976, I came to My Messenger, Sylvia Clarice McChrist, now called Mary-Ma, and gave her Three Dispensations for this upcoming cycle. One was a portrait of Myself as *Mother Mary of the Diamond Heart* (see page 32). The Second Dispensation was an important volume of transformation called *The Keys to the Golden Age*,* which clearly explains the life of My Beloved Son as an exemplary pattern of Initiation for any sincere seekers of Truth.

Humanity follows the Christ, embodies the Christ, passes through His life stages, and finally, like Christ Jesus, ascends from this plane of sorrow. Only now, 24 years after its publication, is the world ready for *The Keys to the Golden Age*, one of the world's first books on ascension!

The Blessed Ascension Rosary was given to all of My beloved children as the Third Dispensation. This new Rosary is the Diamond Key to your own individual ascension (see Chapter 4, The Ascension Process, page 45).

Beloved Lord Mary,
Mother of the Cosmic Christ
Mary Clarice McChrist

---

*This book will soon be revised, enlarged, and republished.

The Blessed Ascension Rosary

Hail Mary, full of Grace,
The Lord is with Thee.
Blessed art Thou among women, and
Blessed is the Fruit of Thy Womb, Jesus.

Holy Mary, Mother of us all,
Blend with us, children of the Sun (Son),*
For we have consciously won our ascension,
Right now and forevermore, I AM!

Beloved Lord Mary,
Mother of the Cosmic Christ

Stanza #1 is the Traditional Rosary given to St. Dominic in 1203.
Stanza #2 was received by Mary Clarice McChrist in 1976, updated in 1993 and 2002.

*Pronounce only once.

Symbolism of the Rosary

I will now interpret the esoteric symbolism of the Rosary Beads for you (see opposite illustration).

The crucifix (1) is the symbol of the Piscean Age during which Our Lord was crucified. The Christian Church has dealt heavily with the suffering and the death of My Son. As the Aquarian or Golden Age is dawning, the emphasis is turning from the crucified figure to the Ascended and victorious Master of Light. It is for this reason that I feel **the figure of Beloved Jesus should not be present on the cross**. His absence implies His victory over death. In all other ways, our beads are organized in the traditional manner.

The initial segment of the Rosary Beads contains a grouping of three beads (3) surrounded on either side by a single larger bead (2). The matrix of three is symbolic of (a) the Father, (b) the Son, and (c) the Divine Mother and Holy Soul. This triad signifies completion of the Christ Matrix upon the Inner or Etheric Planes. The single beads found within the body of the Rosary represent Oneness or God.

The pendulum, or central emblem (4), serves as the heart of the Rosary. My image is frequently represented at this point as the Love Center for the Rosary Beads.

The great Christian Initiations corresponding to the four singular beads (5) have not been taught in this age. These rituals were reserved for the disciples

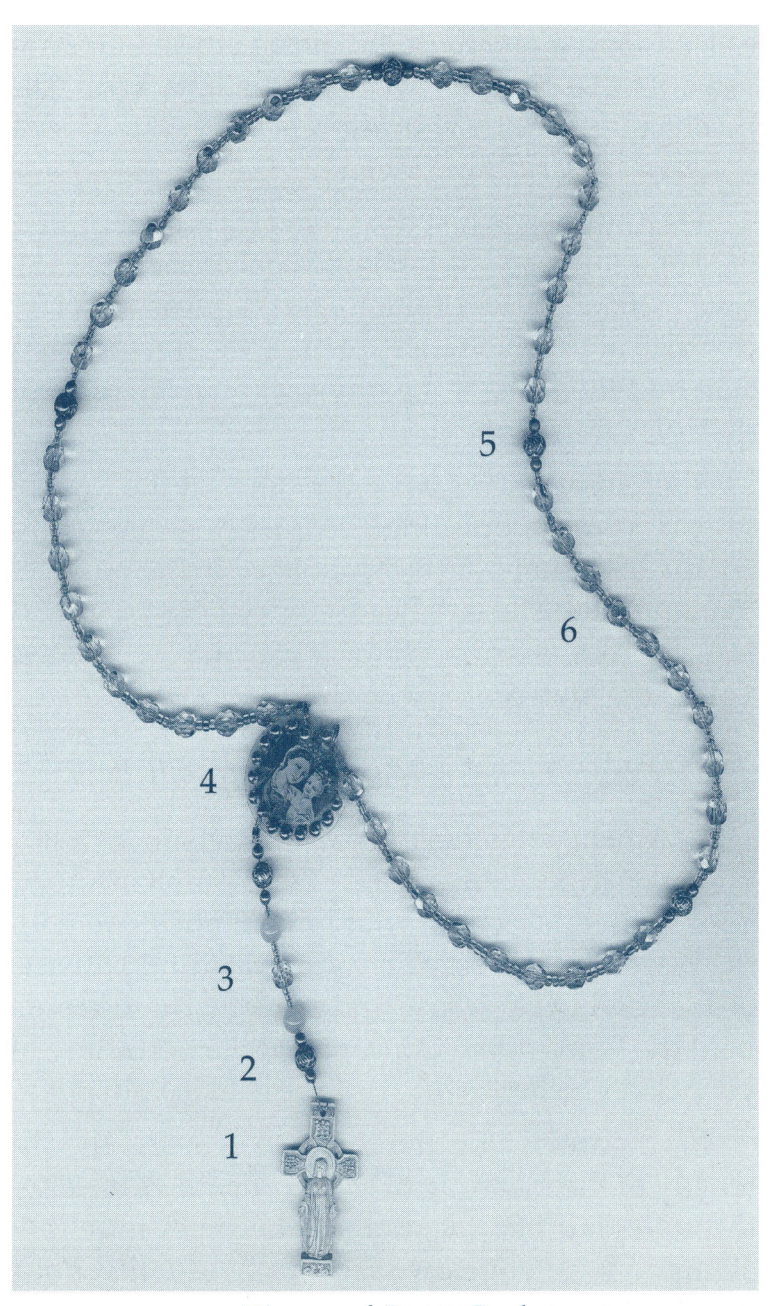

Diagram of Rosary Beads

of Jesus and a few high initiates. I envision the release of these blessed Mystery Initiations when sufficient numbers of you are repeating *The Blessed Ascension Rosary*.

The four beads just discussed (5) are separated by five groupings of ten beads called decants (6). Five is the number of the material quest, descriptive also of the five senses of man, the five-pointed star, and the tests of the physical plane, which all disciples must pass through.

Therefore, as you voice the tones of the Rosary Prayer, you are building the energy necessary to complete the inner tests symbolized in the physical structure of the Rosary Beads. Indeed, the Diamond Key to your own personal ascension is created within the matrix of *The Blessed Ascension Rosary*.

Your Flame of God-Individuality

As you say the Rosary, you are causing a unifying action to occur on several planes simultaneously. Your individuality, and your Inner Light blend with the Words of the Rosary, creating beautiful patterns of Light which are pure and perfect. These words hold the Immaculate Concept and the perfection of your God-Oneness, which is to be held in your heart.

If you are saying the Rosary correctly, the intensity of the meaning of the words flows directly through your heart center and becomes indelibly stamped with your own God-Individuality. Your heart flame also carries within its matrix your personal mission and the Divine Blueprint for your very own ascension. Therefore, *you must always hold to your own unique way of expressing yourself, for your individuality is your precious legacy from God.*

Besides strengthening your personal matrix, the energies of the Rosary Prayer draw the outer self into attunement with your true inner nature, with the Omniscient Energy of God. In this attunement with your own Christ (Illumined Self), Divine Mother, Holy Soul/Spirit, and I Am Presence, the Ascension Flame is literally ignited and expanded within your being.

As the disciple, you will slowly be transformed as you become more successful in losing the hold of the lesser self (ego) upon your life. But *you must never give up your God-Individuality, for each soul has been chosen to amplify a specific aspect of the Divine Mother-Father, which is unique from the mission of all other souls.* Trying to be like someone else never really works.

The Effect of Reciting The Blessed Ascension Rosary

As you say the Rosary, you will be directly connected to My Heart Flame. As you pour forth your Rosary Prayer, the Angelic Hosts will bring to you, from My very Heart, an equal exchange of Light.

Whenever the Rosary is given, healing vibrations cycle off the human voice as the words resound. Mandalas (like etheric energy snowflakes of Light and Love) balance the surrounding environment. Whenever possible, My Light comes forth to illumine

THE COSMIC EIGHT

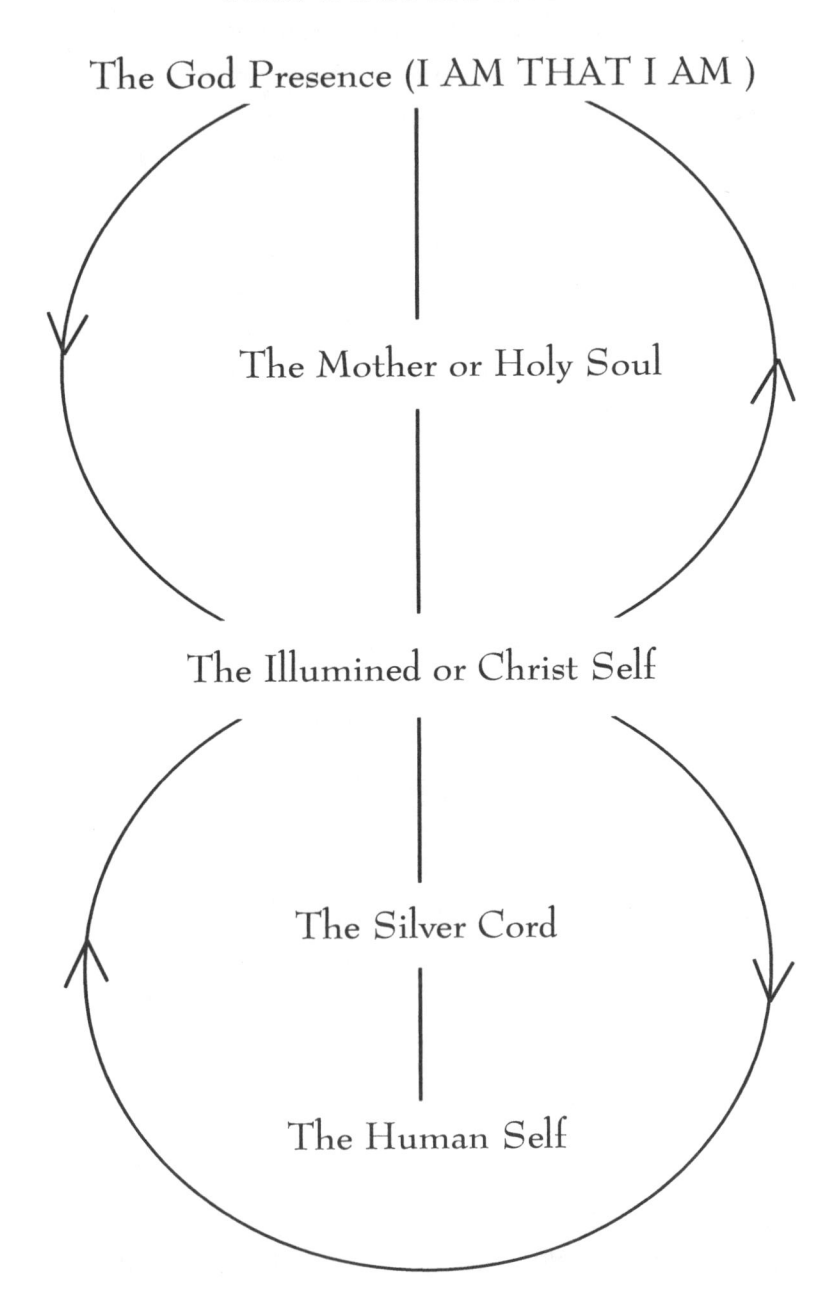

The God Presence (I AM THAT I AM)

The Mother or Holy Soul

The Illumined or Christ Self

The Silver Cord

The Human Self

your being and the world. When there is sickness or sorrow, I come forth, or one of My Ladies come forth, to bring the Peace and Comfort of the Divine Mother.

The Rosary, as previously mentioned, also affects your ascension. The exact pattern of your ascension is also filtering into your etheric body as a Mandala of Light. The energy of the Ascension Flame produced by the Rosary will grow and actually anchor within your heart. The Rosary causes a tremendous influx of light substance within your auric field, connecting as a figure eight with the Christ and the I Am Presence. This is referred to as the Great Cosmic Eight (see chart on page 40). The great cycle of the eight increases your spiritual progress because of the ebbing and flowing exchange of Light and Love within your auric field. These precious energies are used not only for your ascension but for the mission of the Divine Mother and Her Seed.

As your spiritual progress increases, you will find yourselves giving loving service, in one form or another, to all the families and children of the world.

My work is with these lambs, the precious ones of God. As you join with me in giving this Rosary daily, the generated Light shall spread forth across this entire planet.

I Am Mother Mary, Queen of Peace

Mary Clarice McChrist

Claiming Your Ascension, Now

The Blessed Ascension Rosary has been updated to the Now. We must live in the Now, not in the past or the future. Only in the Now can you actively shift reality.

The second stanza of the Rosary Prayer now reflects this incredible and important shift (see underline).

Holy Mary, Mother of us all,

Blend with us, children of the Sun (Son),

<u>For we have consciously won our ascension,</u>

Right now and forevermore, I AM!

Claiming your actual ascension now, is imperative in this Time of Tribulation. Many people will be going Home. Be prepared at any moment for your ascension. Remember, your last moments must be focused on God to Ascend. No matter what, keep your faith.

Support the whole Body of Christ with this precious ascension prayer. As you give this prayer you are telling your subconscious mind that indeed you have ascended; you are an Ascended Master of Light. Every cell and atom of your being must know this Truth.

I Am Mary of Mount Carmel
Mary Clarice McChrist

Chapter 4

The Ascension Process

Lord Jesus - Shroud of Turin Photograph - Touched by Sathya Sai Baba

My Easter Message: "Focus on Ascension"

By Lord Jesus, the Cosmic Christ
April 21, 2000

The Crucifixion drama is not to my liking. It has been blown all out of proportion and focuses on My torture and death.

The Church has used this sequence to control the people in a twisted way. I Am the Son of God, and yet I was crucified. The Church implies that if I, Jesus, the Perfect Son of God, received this treatment, what will a sinner like you receive? In this way, the people are kept in fear.

Enough is enough! Lay this drama aside and remove Me from the cross. Going over and over the crucifixion at Easter causes us all more pain and suffering. Many weep and do penance for Me each year. I came not to die, but to Live and Love, to set forth the Matrix of Resurrection, life after death, as a planetary thoughtform.

The body is a reflection of life. On one level it is very vulnerable and tentative, and yet it houses the Eternal Self, that which never dies and never is born. I came forth to show you that there is NO DEATH. The body is an illusion; reality on Earth is an illusion. By Resurrecting the body, which I did with the help of the Secret Order of the Christ, I set forth the Way.

This Way is now being revealed, for it is now time as we pass from the Piscean Age into the Aquarian Age. The Water Bearer carries the Divine Inspiration which must be drunk to receive the fresh encodements of this time.

I Am the Way, the Truth, and the Life (John 14:6). What does this mean? The Way is the Christ Matrix which I now bring. This is an energy field I alone can give you. It is given only when you have proven who you are to yourself. *When you are God-Realized you take on the whole garment of the Christ.* This means you are now clothed with the substance of Christ. Your blood begins to turn to gold—not the metal—but your dross is transformed through divine alchemy. You become the Golden Christ. You are Christed, for you have followed after Me and passed the Initiations to be Christed. At this point, I Am not outside of you, but I reside within your form. Closer than hands and feet Am I.

The Christ Birth which Christians honor, is the first step of this sevenfold process: Birth, Baptism, Transfiguration, Garden, Crucifixion, Resurrection, and Ascension.

What is Ascension?

Ascension means lifting up beyond material life and consciousness. You can ascend and remain on Earth to give service from within your form. This is the Aquarian way. This is a requirement of the Ascended Christ.

What is Service?

Service allows you to move beyond the limitations of the human ego, to set ego aside, and to give from your Christed Solar Heart. I Am this Heart, and, when you give, expecting nothing in return, your karma (cause and effect) is quickly balanced and erased. This is the fastest Ascension Path.

A gift is always rewarded. When you give to others, you give to Me. Whether you work for Me directly, or you work for Me indirectly through Mary-Ma, you still work for Me.

Service commands the attention of angels. When you do work for Spirit, on behalf of Spirit, more angels are assigned to be with you and to protect you and your loved ones. You gain Magnetic Power and you are able to accomplish more because you have offered yourself unselfishly to God or the Divine Mother. This is Cosmic Law. *No wonder many Avatars—World Teachers and Masters—ask their devotees to give service.*

Ascension as a Group Project

Many do not yet realize that today ascension is largely a group effort. Each Master ascends his/her own Divine Family. These beings are in the same Color Ray Band.

Saint Germain Ascended his helpmates in the 1930's through the 1970's. Some are still following his lead. These dear ones were under the old dispensation in which mastery was completed upon

Earth through initiations and service. Ascension then occurred at the time of death. David Lloyd was able to lift his body in a physical Ascension on the slopes of Mt. Shasta. Mr. Ballard gave David Lloyd an alchemical formula from the Cup of the Holy Grail which had been provided by Master St. Germain (*Unveiled Mysteries*, Godfré Ray King, 1937).

Ascension is now a process rather than an event! There are degrees of ascension into greater and greater levels of the I Am Presence, which culminate with the lifting of the body.

The recent ascension of Miriam Green in Mt. Shasta, CA on March 28, 2000, is a lovely example. This brave lady took on the disease of cancer in order to erase it from human consciousness. She became the focus of individual and group prayer. The people of Mt. Shasta moved beyond any tendency to judge her, to giving her support. The community, especially the women's luncheon group, rallied and supported Miriam in prayer and physical service, while also providing humor and emotional upliftment.

When Miriam left her body, Mother Mary and I met her with others of her Light Council. The energy of the memorial service held in Mt. Shasta was focused by several in form who called for Miriam's ascension. This group energy of music, chanting, and happy recapitulation of special experiences with Miriam was focused in form and could then be amplified by Us in Spirit.

Ascension MUST be called for by one or more people still in the physical plane. When you hear of any death or tragedy upon Earth, always call for the ascension according, to God's Will.

Know, dear ones, you, as a community of God beings, played a vital role in Miriam's ascension. Our thanks are extended to all who participated.

The Divine Ascension Matrix is now anchored in the planetary Christ Grid. However, *a key ingredient is calling: for the ascension by someone in the physical plane.* This establishes the Way for groups to assist in the ascension of their beloved friends. This was an awesome group initiation for the spiritual community of Mt. Shasta. The Way is now set.

My Love and blessings to you each this Easter season.

I Am Lord Jesus, the Cosmic Christ
Mary Clarice McChrist

I Am the Way

I Am the Way
Of the Ascended Christ.
I Am the Path
Leading to the Mount of Shasta.
I Am the Ascension Process.

My Ascension is unfolding daily,
Which is called forth in
The Blessed Ascension Rosary,
Given by Divine Mother Mary.

I Am, through this Rosary,
Establishing the Way of Ascension,
Setting forth the Matrix and Divine Alchemy,
That I shall myself follow.

I Am the Way–
The Ascension into the Heavens,
Manifested through my body and life,
Given through my Ascension Rosary Prayer.

So be it! It is so done!

Lord Jesus, the Cosmic Christ
Mary Clarice McChrist

The Ascension Process

by Lord Mary, Mother of the Cosmic Christ

Defining Ascension

The last stanza of *The Blessed Ascension Rosary* states: "Blend with us children of the Sun (Son), for we have consciously won our ascension right now and forevermore, I AM!"

What is ascension? During the Piscean Age, ascension was the end of the earthly path. The initiate overcame the world by traveling the path exemplified by My Son, Beloved Lord Jesus the Christ. As explained before, each stage of Christ's life outpictured an initiation: the Birth, the Baptism, the Transfiguration, the Garden, the Crucifixion, the Resurrection, and the Ascension. The disciple became the perfected master, balanced his or her karma, and returned to Mother-Father God with his Twin Flame in the ascension. Thus, he or she became an Ascended Being and chose to serve the Earth plane or go on to other expanded forms of service.

Today the situation is different. Ascension no longer means going away, withdrawing from Earth. Instead, it means being totally present in this NOW. *You must descend to ascend!*

As we anchor Heaven on Earth, the complete Essence of who you are comes into your purified physical temple. This means your beloved I Am Presence unifies with your physical form.

The Blessed Ascension Rosary allows you to ascend daily, hourly. You prepare the holy temple, your body, to receive the Christ, the Buddha, the Divine Mother, the Father of Light. You surrender to it All; you become the Allness of the One. Eventually, this Higher Self merges, remaining in an integrated state with the purified human self. You claim your own ascension.

The ascension process occurs on the inner and outer levels, but you may not go anywhere physically. You might very well remain on Earth, serving God and humanity in accordance with your individual mission.

Ascension is also concerned with collective consciousness, the shifting from just an individual focus to group initiations and ascensions. These ascensions will occur in waves as various soul groups come together to birth the Earth into the Golden Age prophesied in the Bible as "1,000 years of Peace, Love, and Harmony."

Presently, individuals are being called together as couples and as soul families. Your present assignment calls for Purification. To aid you in this process, I have brought forth *The Blessed Ascension Rosary* prayer through the Living Flame of My Heart. These devotions reinforce your own ascension and place you under My Mantle of Protection.

I Am Lord Mary
Mary Clarice McChrist

Have You Ascended?

by Lord Jesus, the Cosmic Christ

Ascension is a process, not a singular action. Twenty-one thousand people across Mother Earth ascended on December 12, 1994. Were you one of these people?

Originally, before the Harmonic Convergence in 1987, ascension meant leaving the world of form to serve in the Inner Heavenly Realms. Although this could be a soul choice, it usually now means to serve humanity from the Earth Plane. At the end of this service, the Ascended Master may have earned a Dispensation to raise the body as exemplified 2000 years ago by myself, Christ Jesus, the Way Shower. *This type of Ascension is capitalized.*

Ascension with a small *a* means:

1. You rise above duality, balance male-female polarities within the self, heal the inner child, and you accept and honor the Divine Mother as well as The Father.

2. The transformation of 100% personal karma and world service work for humanity, usually ranging from 5 to 33 years. Later Ascension Waves will not include this requirement.

3. You must be involved in your personal mission and have taken Bodhisattva Vows, at least on the Inner Planes. This is a personal commitment to serve until all beings ascend with our planet.

4. Your normal 2-strand DNA pattern will become a DNA of twelve strands. This will have first occurred for many Light workers December 31, 1994, at approximately 4 PM PST, during the World Healing Day when prayers for Global Peace criss-crossed our planet. This process will continue.
5. The level of your work is increased by the initial Ascension Process. New Ascended Beings may now work from levels 5–17 on the Inner Planes.
6. You are now considered a Probationary Ascended Master. Levels of mastery and growth never stop. The highest masters continue to evolve and expand their areas of service to humanity and the entire cosmos.
7. You have the awesome responsibility to wield your authority with Humility, Compassion, and Love. *What an Ascended Master thinks, says, or commands, manifests quickly in this world of form.*
8. There is a fine line, a middle way, of living, serving, and co-creating with friends, community, and the world.
9. What you focus upon, you become.
10. What you give to others is returned to you magnified ten-thousand fold.

As you can see, ascension is not to be rushed into for it carries tremendous responsibility. Lord Jesus explained, "... my burden is light." (Matthew 11:30)

This Light is the Ascension. If you have ascended, you will know it. The requirements will have been met. Your entire being will say, "Yes, I AM an Ascended Master. It is so done!" You may receive chills or your personal confirmation signal as you read these words.

I Am Lord Jesus, the Cosmic Christ
Mary Clarice McChrist

Service and Ascension
by Lord Jesus, the Cosmic Christ

One way of understanding ascension is to say that you move from the mind to the heart, from a human being to becoming a Divine Christed Master. Instead of withdrawing from the Earth, you may stay and perform Divine Service for the planet. There are many ways this Service may be expressed, for each person is unique. Look around; it is pretty obvious who is ascended. Is the life of the person dedicated to the world and Spirit, or is it dedicated to the small self? Look at the fruits.

Your Personal Mission

The Great Ones call some people to play leadership roles and others are called to support organizations or individuals by offering some sort of assistance. Some people wish to help, but they have no idea of what to do. Can you do data entry? Could you prepare a book for publication? Could you help build or maintain the garden for Our Lady of all Nations? Could you donate flowers for the garden? Can you be of service to Mary-Ma or others?

Go into your heart of Hearts and commune with your Higher Self. What is my mission? Can I purify myself by giving service? Will I be in a supportive or leadership role? Could I be a networker in my area for Mother Matrix events? What can I give?

Some individuals are gifted with financial abundance.

Your mission may be to financially give to individuals or organizations you feel called upon to support. Being a financial angel is a high calling. Pray to be guided in your life, your mission, and in all service that you give. "Not my will but thine be done."

The Inner Plane Ascension Ritual

Ascension is a process, not a single act or stage you pass through. There are levels of ascension. When a Probationary Ascended Master in form is finally called Home, you go through a very special ritual on the inner levels.

You as a Master are accompanied by your Twin Flame. The couple stands before the Ascension Tribunal and is asked to speak of your world service accomplishments. Other Ascended Ones may also speak on your behalf. (Yogis and some individuals who have lived in caves or in isolation have performed a unique type of service. They do not give service in the normal way. They *are* the service, for they are living Embodiments of God. You are also this.)

The Tribunal reaches a decision, and the Ascension Process ensues. The Great Ascension Flame is passed through the Twins. The bodies have been preparing for this awesome moment for lifetimes. All less than the purest Christ Light vanishes; not one erg of darkness remains. The Twins stand whole, complete, as dazzling Ascended Masters of Light.

The Heavens and Earth rejoice. A great party on

the Inner Planes is manifested to celebrate this wondrous occasion. All Earth and all humanity is raised up by this individual ascension. *May I be with you on the Sacred Day you win your Victory over this world.* May I be the first one to come forth and greet you as a new Ascended Master of Light.

I Am Your Brother in the Flame,

Lord Jesus, the Cosmic Christ

Mary Clarice McChrist

Chapter 5

World Service Devotions

Mary Speaks on the Power of Prayer

Prayer is vital for relationships, marriage, children, your place of worship—church, temple, synagogue or nature, your country, and Beloved Mother Gaia.

The purpose of prayer is:

> To establish communication between yourself and Mother-Father God.
>
> To give praise and thanks for the good already received.
>
> To seek help with personal healing, clearing, and transmutation.
>
> To request or petition the Creator for His/Her Direct Intervention.

The tradition in which you choose to pray is up to you. I would not move you from your truth. If you are without a spiritual practice, dear one, then I invite you to use the Gifts I have given for this time of transition. They are: *The Blessed Ascension Rosary*, *The Blessed Mother's Blue Rose of the Healing Heart*, and *The Keys to the Golden Age*.

Dearest children, prayer is your powerful ally. I call you to prayer. Know I stand by your side as you recite the prayers from My books or those prayers found on the Mother Matrix Web Site : www.mother-matrix.org. Realize it is important for us to connect directly and powerfully so that you will know the Protection and Safety of My Grace.

Dear beloved ones, My Heart flows out to you and enfolds you. We are One Heart! My Son, Blessed Christ Jesus, is one with our hearts. We melt together into Bliss—the Flame of Divine Love.

We call you forth to heal yourself and to heal your families. Stand firm against opposition which would shatter marriage and break up family units.

Pray for all people. Pray for each other. Please make this dedication with the Flaming Hearts of Mary and Jesus. Say *The Blessed Ascension Rosary* and *The Rosary of Tribulation* daily.

The Tribulation is at hand. Those who are weak will not be able to stand against the waves of misfortune. I desire the well-being of each one of My children upon this planet!

As you pray for all people in the Blue Rose World Service Groups or at home individually, you strengthen the grid work of the Mother Matrix. This invisible garment of the Divine Mother is being formed in, through, and around the Christ Grid to strengthen and link humanity to Divine Love.

I Am Your Mother, Queen of Peace

Mary Clarice McChrist

Mary Speaks on Your Daily Prayer Ritual

It is essential at this Time of Tribulation to create or continue a daily spiritual practice.

I created *The Blessed Mother's Blue Rose of the Healing Heart* for this purpose. This precious book is also the foundation of the *Blue Rose World Service Groups*.

Read through the first section of this book to obtain vital background information. In Chapter 5, *World Service Devotions*, and Chapter 8, *Winning the Protection Game*, the prayers of Lord Michael enfold you in the Blue Flame of the Son.

As you call Archangel Michael, He goes before you cleansing your daily path from all that is less than the purest Christ Light. Daily, put on the Whole Armor of God, and then walk in Peace!

The Blue Rose Prayers are carefully designed to bring you into Spiritual Union. The goal is to go inside, not outside, to gain your spiritual strength. *As you pray the new Ascension Rosary, I come into Oneness with you. In this age, Christ Jesus has said, "I and My Mother are One!"*

You will become stronger and stronger in your abilities to meet the challenges of the day. Know that you are never alone. Christ and I are with you. Your guardian angels never leave your side. Your personal Council of Light, your Spiritual Teachers, and your personal etheric guides are close at hand (See *Spiritual Evaluations*, p. 241). Know you are protected and reside within My Heart.

Mary Speaks on Faith

Behold, My Children,

I call you to Faith. I call you to open to Me, not with your mind, for the mind may be stuck in its own tiny box of restrictions. I call you to commune with your heart. Open your heart.

Can you believe that My tears flow from statues? Can you allow the possibility that some statues of Me move at My Will? Can you believe miracles and healings occur for many of My children?

Dear Ones, this world is filled with disbelief. How sad! I Am your Mother. I call you to Faith. The need to prove scientifically every Miracle I perform in the Name of My Son Jesus shows the sad state of disbelief in God. It is for this reason that I cry.

Dear faithful ones, hold fast. Stay under My protection. Allow Me to draw you into My Flaming Heart. *Say the Rosary daily. Recite the Rosary for Me, for yourself, and do this for our beloved planet.*

With Unified Faith, we can shift and dissolve the rigidity of mental constructs, which must be melted for God-Goddess to flow effortlessly throughout the people of Earth.

I call this forth now!

I Am Mary, Mother of Christ Jesus
Mary Clarice McChrist

Prayer of Unified Faith

Have Faith in the Father, the Son,
and the Holy Ghost.

Have Faith in the unity of
the Flaming Hearts of Jesus and Mary.

Have Faith in the Blesssd Ascension Rosary
as it purifies all lands and all peoples.

Have Faith that Christ Jesus
overcame death and disease.

Have Faith that the Son was Resurrected,
thus reversing the hold of death.

Have Faith that the Son was lifted up in the
Ascension unto the Father's Right Hand.

Have Faith that the Path of Christ Jesus
is the Path of all believers, regardless
of their religious persuasions.

For all Paths are founded upon Faith,
good works, and growth, through the
expansion of the heart.

These qualities may be hidden, yet they are
present in all Paths that lead eventually to
the one great I AM THAT I AM.

Buddha directs you toward Enlightenment.

Krishna offers Beauty and Bliss.

Moses brings the Law of God.

Christ offeres the Heart.

It is a personal choice as to which Path is right for an individual soul.

I Am Mother Mary,
Queen of Peace
Mary Clarice McChrist

World Service Prayer

Blessed Madonna and Christ Child Jesus,
Open my heart, my eyes, my voice.
Help me daily to give the Rosary.
Blaze the Three-Fold Flames of my heart,
That I might join the world servers,
Whose Flaming Hearts surround
The entire Earth.

Sweet Lord Mary and Child of the Christos,
Please open the hearts of all people.
Let us kneel together in fearless victory,
Faithfully joining in this world prayer–
That the Time of the Great Tribulation
Shall be eased, that the Rosary be given,
That the people will earnestly seek God
And the Protection of Archangel Michael.

Mother Mary, Queen of Peace
Mary Clarice McChrist

My Family Prayer

Holy Christ family,
Divine Father-Mother God,
Manifest for my personal children
Complete freedom from separation,
Disease, and death.
Keep my human family safe
Now in this time of transition.
Gather us together, within
The Immaculate Heart of Mary.
There may we remain untouched,
Forevermore, I Am!

Blessed be Lord Mary,
Mother of God

AUM (All United in Mary) (3x)
Mary Clarice McChrist

Divine Mercy for Our Ancestors

Divine Mercy for my ancestors.
Family of our mother and father,
Those whose name I carry,
Those whose blood runs within my veins,
We honor you and bless your lives eternally.

Divine Mercy for my ancestors.
May my DNA replicate Christ's blood.
May I synthesize all great Lines of Purity
And release dis-ease or tendencies for karmas
Which might fall into my family lineage.

In honoring you, dear family, I request
That the Divine Matrix of the family
Align with my True Mission
And that the family be supportive of my destiny.

In this time of transition, it is appropriate
To cleanse our family name of all
Separation from God Father-Mother,
To open to Divinity for this holy family.

Blessed Christ Jesus and Mother Mary,
Open the Portals of Heaven for my ancestors,
Lifting each member into the Ascension Flame,
Creating a momentum for all of my lineage.

Transport me, Dear Mother and Son,
To the feet of the Most Holy Lord of Hosts.
In the Flame and Fires of Purity raise me
In the hour of my ascension from this plane.

Lift me up with my body into the Light Supreme.
Archangels, come and stand about me holding sway
Over all phases of my ascension.
Blessed Great Father, call me to Your Side.

For I Am One with Christ your Son.
Ancestors, witness my ascension,
Even with my dear Mother Lord Mary,
For She promises to guide me
To the Most High Throne.

For God, Thou art my Redeemer,
And Thy Grace is with me evermore.
Amen, Ah-women, Ah-child, All One!

The Triad Speaks

Mary Clarice McChrist

Lord Michael

In the Name of my Holy Christ Self, the Holy Christ Selves of all humankind, my own Beloved I Am Presence, Archangels Michael and Faith, the Fathers and the Mothers of the Rays, Beloved Lanello and Godfré, Beloved Mother Principles, I decree:

1. Lord Michael, my friend,
   Blaze forth the trend
   For freedom to be
   Saint Germain-free.* (**3x)

Refrain:

> O come, come now,
> To Truth I vow.
> Protect us all.
> To Thee I call.

2. Lord Michael, Great One,
   My Blue, Radiant Son.
   Thy Sword and Thy Shield
   Make all evil yield. (3x)

3. Lord Michael and Faith,
   Blaze forth the pace.
   Reunion be One
   My own I AM Son. (3x)

4. Lord Michael, I'm free
   From all less than Thee.
   Protected and sealed
   Thy Blue Faith revealed! (3x)

5. Lord Michael, my family be
   Protected and sealed by Thee
   Until all the souls of men
   In Ascension Fire surely blend. (3x)

By the Power of Divine Love, I agree, together with Lord Jesus the Christ, "Where two or more are gathered in My Name, there AM I!"

By the Light and Might of my own I AM,

It is sealed! It is sealed! It is sealed!

Beloved I AM! (3x)

Beloved Djwhal Khul
Mary Clarice McChrist

---

* *as free as Lord St. Germain*
** *3x — notation indicates repeat 3 times.*

Tube of Light
(stand)

Beloved Mighty Victorious Presence of God I AM in me; Alpha and Omega in the Great Central Sun; Luminous Helios and Vesta in the Sun of our system; Beloved Omritas, ruler of the Violet Planet; Mighty Victory; Beloved Karmic Board; Beloved Sanat Kumara; Lady Master Venus; Beloved Pallas Athena; Lord El Morya; Beloved Maha Chohan; Beloved Lord Gautama; Lord Mary Buddha; Beloved Hilarion; Beloved Mighty Astrea; Beloved Lord Michael and the Legions of Light; Beloved Lord Mary; Lord Jesus, the Cosmic Christ; and the entire Spirit of the Great Council of Light, I decree:

1. Beloved I AM Presence bright,
   Round me seal your Tube of Light.
   I Am acting with full God-Power.
   Acting here this time, this hour. (3x)

2. Beloved I AM Presence bright,
   Fill the Tube with Violet Light.
   Burning dross, transmuting tears,
   Melting karma of all the years. (3x)

3. Holy I AM Presence bright,
   Round me seal the Tube of Light.
   Violet Fire consume, sustain,
   Blaze until no dross remains. (3x)

Coda: Melt self away, melt self away. (6x)
Freedom shall stay. (6x)
Victory God's way! (6x)

By the Power of Divine Love, I agree, together with Lord Jesus the Christ, "Where two or more are gathered in My Name, there AM I!"

By the Light and Might of my own I AM,

It is sealed! It is sealed! It is sealed!

Beloved I AM! (3x)

Lord El Morya of Cosmic Divine Will
Mary Clarice McChrist

Additional Protection:

I call my I AM Presence to place me in seven nested Capsules of Light, each at arms length from the last Capsule.

Feel the security of this action.

Auric Safety Decree
(especially recommended for children)

I call on Jesus the Christ. (3x)
Bubble of Light, (3x)
Seal me tight (3x)
With God's Might. (3x)
It is done! (3x)
We are One! (3x)
Right now, with full God-power!
Beloved I Am! (3x)

Lord El Morya
Mary Clarice McChrist

Personal Protection from Archangel Michael

Lord Michael, descend,
Descend unto this plane.
Clear and circulate throughout my world,
Placing a sphere of Cosmic Protection
Above, below, around, and through myself,
My family, my property, home,
Work place, and school.

Oversee our daily lives and travels.
Encircle my car with your protective light.
Protect me and my loved ones during transit.
Clear mechanical objects
That they might work properly
According to God's Holy Will.

Allow no vibration of turmoil,
Confusion, or tribulation to touch me
Or my beloved loved ones.
For we are children of the Sun (Son)*
Whole, perfect, reflecting
The Immaculate Concept of Being.
Thank you, Beloved Lord Michael.
Beloved I Am! (3x)

Lord Michael
Mary Clarice McChrist

---

*Prounce only once.

Invocation For Ascension

I invoke the Power of the Great Central Sun
In, under, and through my body temple.
May the Fires of the Holy City, Foursquare,
Inspire and replenish my soul.

May the Powers of the Councils of Light
Be focused within my being
And hereby establish Perfection,
Power, and Truth in my Eternal Presence.

I live and move and have my being
To express my Holy God Plan.
I Am directed in speech and action
From my Presence to my human self.

I release my ego goals, ambitions, and dreams
To Thy Holy Will.
I release any personal selfish interests
To join in the Greater Group Work.

To lift man to his God-Potential
And also to the goal:
To commune, blend, and strengthen the bonds
Of brotherhood between all humankind.

To move up the Path of Discipleship
Toward the mastery of the lower planes.
To conquer all the wayward paths
And yet press on, press on,
Toward the completion of my ascension.

This is my way, my life, my plan.
I will obtain my goal. I will. I can! (3x)

Archangel Jophiel,
Yellow Ray of Wisdom

Mary Clarice McChrist

Ascension Fire Decree

Serapis Bey, Luxor Retreat,
May I visit at your feet?
Ascension Flame, O now begin,
Blaze through, and back again.

Chorus:

Serapis Bey, descend White Fire,
Blazing Flame of God's Desire.
Bring the Ascension Flame to me.
Blaze it through and cut me free!

Mastery we gain each hour,
Humbly, we serve the Power.
Like white-robed Masters of the Light,
We raise ourselves beyond Earth's plight.

With our Twin, we stand at last,
Ascension Tribunal checks our past.
What Service have you given Earth,
To ascend this night, beyond rebirth?

So stand we now, with Purity ring,
Ascension Flame through us does sing.
O free at last, the Heavens rejoice,
Let Ascension be the whole world's choice.

Serapis Bey
Mary Clarice McChrist

Chapter 6
Blue Rose Prayers

Mary with Rosary - Scottsdale Apparition Photogrph

The Blessed Mother's Blue Rose of the Healing Heart

Rosary Instructions

1. Call in Lord Mary:
   "Beloved Lord Mary, come forth." (3x)
2. Read aloud for greatest power: *Mary is with You.*
3. Read *Message from Lord St. Germain.*
4. Read *Mary's Promise to Her Children.*
5. Read the *Blue Rose Prologue.*
6. Read *Matrix of the Mother.*
7. Read aloud for groups:
   A World Dispensation and *Protection and Purity.*
8. Read *Your Rosary Beads.*
9. *The Rosary of Tribulation.* Hold beads to your heart.
10. Recite *Our Mother's Prayer* for the 1st large bead.
11. Call for the Holy Spirit with the giving of *O Dove of Peace* for the next three beads.
12. Call upon the Father with the recitation of *The Lord's Prayer* for the 2nd large bead.
13. Anchor the prayer momentum with the "AUM"..
14. Give *Mary's Communion Prayer* at the Heart Medal.

15. Recite *The Blessed Ascension Rosary* (5 -10x) on the 1st sets of 10 beads (decant), after the prayer.
16. Read *Lord Mary's Call*, large bead, end of 1st decant.
17. Say *The Blessed Ascension Rosary*, 2nd decant (5 -10x).
18. Recite *The Prayer for the Beloved Children*, (large bead).
19. Give *The Rosary for the Inner Child*, 3rd decant (5-10x).
20. Say *Prayer for the Transmutation of World Sorrow*, 3rd decant.
21. Recite *The Black Madonna Rosary*, 4th decant (5-10x).
22. Give *The Immaculate Concept Prayer*, end of 4th decant.
23. *The Blessed Ascension Rosary*, fifth decant, (recite 9x) and *Conclusion of the Rosary* (1x).
24. Recite *I Am Your Mother* on Heart Medal.
25. Give *Increasing the Rosary Momentum*, hold beads.
26. *Sign of the Cross*, move beads with words of the prayer.
27. Completion and Blessing, give the *Closing Prayer*.
28. *Cosmic Mother's Sealing Prayer*, end of individual prayer session.
29. Hear or sing *the Ave Maria* song or CD.
30. Sing the *I Am Presence Song*.
31. Hear a channeling from Mother Mary (order cassette tape from: www.mother-matrix.org).
32. Read *Lord Mary's Request*.
33. Give *Mary's Rose Crusade for World Peace*.

Blue Rose Prayers

1. Attunement to Mary.

    Say aloud:

    "Beloved Lord Mary, come forth." (3x)*
    * indicates repeat 3 times.

2. Hold the Rosary Beads and read *Mary Is With You!*

Mary Is With You

Your Mother is here to give comfort,
To hold you in My Arms
As I held My Son, Jesus.

Adult or child, I hold you.
Cry in My Arms—let go.
Call out for help; it is time.
I Am with you now.
Ask for the Mother's Grace.
Together we can pass through.

In this time of great pressure,
When the old world and its ways
Shift and dissolve around you,
Be not afraid, the angels are here.
Lord Michael swings His Sword before you,

Cutting free the patterns that hold.
Ascending dimension by dimension,
Beyond density, chaos, and
Illusion of the darkness,
Know the bright world is coming soon.

Hold on, My little ones; know that I Am here.
Saint Germain brings his Violet Flame
To transmute all less than Christ Purity.

Blue of Father God, Pink of the Mother,
Invisible God-Action in perfect balance.
O Violet Flame, bathe all My sweet children.

I lift from humanity all violence and pain.
I bring the precious Gift, the Rosary Prayer,
That you, My children, might be at Peace.

Knowing the travail of Earth is at hand,
<u>Pray, be thankful, forgive, forgive, forgive,
Even as the Father and I forgive you all.</u>

Call Me, cry with Me, allow the flow.
As rain purifies the Earth, let go.
Let your Love and Joy flow to all life.
I Am your Mother. Together we can win.

I Am Lord Mary,
Mother of the Cosmic Christ

Mary Clarice McChrist

3. Share the *Message from Lord St.Germain.*

Message from Lord SaintGermain

The giving of the Rosary creates a protective forcefield over the prayerful person and throughout the immediate environment. This Holy Matrix is infused with God-Peace and Divine Order. Such atmosphere causes great soul growth to occur.

When The Blessed Ascension Rosary is given widely enough, this momentum of the Love and Light of the Divine Mother will create a transforming effect, causing a Planetary Light Link to occur. Outmoded patterns will melt away, and the new Ascension Vibration will bring hope and healing to an otherwise burdened planet.

Beloved, know also that **The Blessed Ascension Rosary is given not for Mary but for yourself**—for your personal ascension, your protection during earth changes, your healing, and growth into the wholeness of your God-Being—for the complete ascension requires the anchoring of the Beloved I AM Presence into your physical form. The recitation of *The Blessed Ascension Rosary* is a personal choice for freedom, an individual contribution toward the healing of Mother Earth. My blessings are upon those beings who have chosen to make this dedication toward Lord Mary's work in this age.

I Am Lord Saint Germain,
Cosmic Christ of the Violet Flame

Mary Clarice McChrist

4. Read *Lord Mary's Promise to Her Children.*

Lord Mary's Promise to Her Children

I ask that *The Blessed Ascension Rosary* be given before an image of Myself, the Blessed Mother, the Black Madonna, or the Goddess. These serve as a Matrix of Light which focuses My Presence into the room.

Whatever children wish to make this dedication with Me shall inherit the New Kingdom and shall be called the Blessed Children of the Immaculate Heart of Mary.

I make this Covenant with these, My children. If you center in your hearts and give *The Blessed Ascension Rosary* faithfully each day, you shall not translate* before your ascension is fully anchored within your four lower bodies. Further, in this time of the great Tribulation, not a hair upon your head shall be touched.

This is my promise to you, that you might be prepared and sanctified by My Hand.

I Am Lord Mary,
Mother of the Cosmic Christ

Mary Clarice McChrist

---

*Leave the body in death.

5. Read the *Blue Rose Prologue.*

Blue Rose Prologue

Beloved Children:

I see about me such pain:
Pain inflicted one upon another,
Heaviness in the heart,
Suffering, like that of the Crucifixion
Of the Beloved Lord Jesus, My Son.

It is not meant that you in form
Should suffer such pain.
The accumulated debt of world sin—
Separation from God—
Lays heavily upon the hearts of saints.

For it is the pure in heart
Who feel much pain
That is not truly yours.
For the atonement of sin, which is
Separation from God,
Draws to you to be lifted off,
Through your own prayers.

This process called spiritual alchemy
Has been taught in secret for centuries.

I Am Lord Mary

Mary Clarice McChrist

6. Give the explanation for *Matrix of the Mother*.

Matrix of the Mother

Now, Dear Ones,

I give unto you the Matrix of the Mother.
The Mother Matrix is the Mother's
Divine Grid Work of Consciousness
Which is interwoven with the Christ Grid.

For you have now earned
Complete resonance and protection by daily
Reciting My Blue Rose Prayers.

I now flow through Myself,
In the form of Mary Clarice McChrist,
My Voice, My Touch, My Field of Light,
My Mantle of Cosmic Protection.
Let this be a Covenant between us all
That I Am with you,
And you are One with Me
In complete Oneness and Trust.

I and My Father are One.
I and My Mother are One.
This is the Mantra of the New Day!
Adopt this now as your personal mantra.

I Am Lord Mary,
Mother of the Cosmic Christ

Mary Clarice McChrist

7. Read the Explanation of *The Rosary of Tribulation* and *Protection and Purity.*

A World Dispensation

Beloved Archangel Raphael came to Mary-Ma McChrist and offered her a <u>six-minute</u> World Service Dispensation Prayer called the *Rosary of Tribulation.*

A Dispensation is a special Gift from Spirit. This prayer is a lovely short practice which may be given separately or concurrently with the *Blue Rose Ascension Rosary Prayers.*

T*he Rosary of Tribulation* specifically addresses world's problems. It instantly allows the transmutation of each issue with the *Hail Mary* chorus of *The Blessed Ascension Rosary,* which is the Heart of My Teachings. This is a truly profound practice.

I Am Lord Mary,
Mother of the Cosmic Christ

Mary Clarice McChrist

Protection and Purity

Devotees have successfully utilized this prayer for exorcisms, as well as for a daily world prayer practice.

The phrase, "the Milk of the Holy Mother" is as powerful as calling for "the Blood of Jesus", which created a Christ barrier of protection for the disciple. The Milk is the Colostrum of the Divine Mother. This is My Living Essence and I freely offer this Dispensation of Nurturing and Protection to you and to all of My beloved, sweet children.

The Rosary of Tribulation explains My Divine Authority within the cosmos. I Am very grateful for those of you who wish to offer this powerful prayer in your daily prayer rituals.

I am Lord Mary,
Mother of the Cosmic Christ

Mary Clarice McChrist

Mary in Italy
Apparition - Photographer Unknown

8. Read *Your Rosary Beads.*

Your Rosary Beads

The Rosary may be recited with or without the Rosary Beads. If you wish to utilize the beads, please follow exact instructions given before each prayer.

Rosary Beads may be purchased through the Mother Matrix Web Site: **www.mother-matrix.org** or from any Catholic bookstore.

Please remember to **remove Jesus from the cross, as we are focusing on His Ascension rather than His suffering and death.** We are transmuting all past illusions and forgiving all for their actions.

As you pray, your beads will become charged with your prayer momentum. They may be worn around your neck for special protection. Know you are the children of My Heart. Ask Mother to bless your beads.

I Am Mary

Mary Clarice McChrist

9. Pray *The Rosary of the Tribation*. Charge the beads with your heart.

The Rosary of Tribulation

Hail Mary

Hail Mary, full of Grace,
The Lord is with Thee.
Blessed art Thou among women, and
Blessed is the Fruit of Thy Womb, Jesus.

Holy Mary, Mother of us all,
Blend with us, children of the Sun (Son),*
For we have consciously won our Ascension,
Right now and forevermore, I AM.

Bless all humans, formed and unformed.

Hail Mary

Bless Mary's children who are in the throes of Tribulation.

Hail Mary

Bless beings in despair, lack or sorrow.

Hail Mary

Bless beings who are hungry, homeless, or dying.

Hail Mary

Bless beings as they transcend darkness into Light.

Hail Mary

Bless those who choose to withdraw from life.

---

*Pronounce only once.

Hail Mary

Bless Mary's dedicated children who remain under the protection of the Milk of the Holy Mother.

Hail Mary

Blessed is Mary, feminine Lord of Our Universe, Mother of Our Cosmos, Protector of the Innocent.

Hail Mary

Blessed Mother, translate all sorrow, enfold us as children in Your Tender Arms.

Hail Mary

May we drink Your Milk of Compassion.

Hail Mary

For Mother, You hold our Divine Blueprint, our perfect identity, our emotional stability, our clarity of mind. Open our compassion, tenderness, and ability to love and strengthen others.

Hail Mary

Holy Mother, we are as babes in Your Arms, Comforted, Protected, and at Peace.

I Am ascended! (3x)

A-men, Ah-women, Ah-child, All-One.

Blessed Ascension Rosary by Beloved Lord Mary
Rosary of Tribulation by Archangel Raphael
Mary Clarice McChrist

10. Call forth the Supreme Mother by reciting on first large bead.

Our Mother's Prayer

Our Mother of the Void,
Of the Earth and of the Heaven,
Our Mother, Divine, deep darkness,
Holy Womb of all Creation,

O Supreme Mother of all form,
Life, gunas, kayas, and realities,
Source of all birth, death, resurrection, and ascension,
Weaver of the webs, the dimensions, and
The Cycles of Eternity,
Mother, we bow to Thee and
Open our hearts in reverence.

In surrender, we watch Thy Wonders,
The Gods and Goddesses of all religions
Flowing forth from Your Beingness.
Your Nature is black, sweet goodness,
Pure water and Cosmic Fire.
You are both the destroyer in nature
And nurturer in form.

With awe, we see the turning of Your cycles,
Your seasons, Your rhythms of life.
Through the sun-star-Earth, You descend
Into form, into the heart of Earth,
And then, You return form to Spirit.

Holy is Thy Name, O Supreme Mother.
Bless, Heal, Nurture, and Protect Your children.
In Supreme Mother we Trust.

Mary Clarice McChrist

11. Call the Holy Spiri by reciting this on beads 2, 3, and 4. (3x)

O Dove of Peace

O Dove of Peace, descend,
Descend upon our hearts.

O Dove of Peace, transcend,
Transcend all less than Thou Art.

O Dove of Peace, blend,
Blend, we are now Divine.

O Dove of Peace, send,
Send God's Son and His Design.

Beloved Lord Jesus, the Cosmic Christ
Mary Clarice McChrist

12. Call forth the Father; recite on second large bead.

The Lord's Prayer

Our Father, which art in Heaven,
(O Father-Mother God, Divine Oneness.)

Hallowed be Thy Name.
(Glory to our own Beloved I Am Presence.)

Thy Kingdom come,
(Father, bring forth the Golden Age.)

Thy will be done on Earth, as it is in Heaven.
(For the New Age of Peace and brotherhood is completed, even now, on the Inner Planes.)

Give us this day our daily bread.
(Supply our needs as they manifest.)

And forgive us our debts, as we forgive our debtors.
(For love is reflected in love.)

And lead us not into temptation, but deliver us from evil.
(Mother-Father God, help us to remain in the Temple of the Absolute, beyond the experience of maya.)

For Thine is the Kingdom, and the Power,
and the Glory, forever.
(For Thou art now, the Golden Age, manifested within the Immaculate Perfect Image of Man. Right now, and forevermore!)

AUM (All United in Mary) (3x)

Holy Bible (Matthew 6:9-13): *The New Lord's Prayer*

Beloved Jesus, the Cosmic Christ

Mary Clarice McChrist

13. Group Leader Reads:

"Use the AUM energy to anchor each section."

ॐ

AUM

A = All. Gathering the prayer energies.

U = United. Pass the energies through your body.

M = in Mary. Consciously move the Light down through yourself deep into the crystal core of Mother Earth.

Read to the Group: "Know that you are now integrated with this new level of Self. Your Rainbow Body, or Light Body is created by each erg of positive energy that you release."

14. Recite prayer at the Heart Medal. One person reads to the group.

Mary's Communion Prayer

Beloved Ones,

I come this day to enter into
Communion with you on a personal basis.
I will come as you recite these prayers.
I will impress upon your hearts and minds
Suggestions which will help transmute
Your problems and the issues of those about you.

Create an atmosphere of Peace,
Serenity, and Divine Order
In your home and environment.
As we hold the Immaculate Concept
For ourselves and Beloved Mother Earth,
Many hearts must consciously join together
In prayer, fasting, and goodwill to *all life*.
We must Love all life as the Mother.

The Crucible of Man is the Christ/Buddhic family.
These Avatars inherited the souls of this planet.
I cannot separate one from the other.
For God's Holy Blessing is upon all life.
We honor all spiritual expressions of God.

I Am Lord Mary,
Cosmic Mother of the Christos

Mary Clarice McChrist

15. The first decant (Repeat 5 - 10x). Group may recite (2x or 3x).

The Blessed Ascension Rosary

Hail Mary, full of Grace,
The Lord is with Thee.
Blessed art Thou among women, and
Blessed is the Fruit of Thy Womb, Jesus.

Holy Mary, Mother of us all,
Blend with us, children of the Sun (Son),
For we have consciously won our ascension,
Right now and forevermore, I AM!

Beloved Lord Mary,
Mother of the Cosmic Christ

Stanza #1 is the Traditional Rsary given to St. Dominic in 1203.
Stanza #2 was received by Mary Clarice McChrist in 1976, updated in 1993 and 2002.

16. Recite at the end of the first decant, large bead.

Lord Mary's Call

O children, come to the Mother.
- C* because I love you,
- O because you need comfort and rest,
- M because your hearts need to open.
- E

O children, come to the Mother.
- Y* journey has held tragedy,
- O hearts need to open,
- U tears need to flow.
- R

O children, come to the Mother.
- T*
- H is healing in my aura,
- E is comfort in my arms,
- R is Love which melts all sorrow.
- E

O Children, come!

* Read the word 'come,' 'your,' or 'there' before each phrase.

I Am Lord Mary

Mary Clarice McChrist

17. The second decant (Repeat 5-10x). Group may recite (2x or 3x).

The Blessed Ascension Rosary

Hail Mary, full of Grace,
The Lord is with Thee.
Blessed art Thou among women, and
Blessed is the Fruit of Thy Womb, Jesus.

Holy Mary, Mother of us all,
Blend with us, children of the Sun (Son),
For we have consciously won our ascension,
Right now and forevermore, I AM!

Beloved Lord Mary
Mother of the Cosmic Christ

Stanza #1 is the Traditional Rosary given to St. Dominic in 1203.
Stanza #2 was received by Mary Clarice McChrist in 1976, updated in 1993 and 2002.

Madonna of the Street
by Roberto Ferrussi

18. Recite at the end of the second decant, large bead. Group or on person may recite.

Prayer for the Beloved Children

O Blessed Mary, Mother of God,
I pray with Your Holy Child Jesus
For the protection of all children,
For the inner child-self of all adults,
For the healing and nurturing of the child.
I call that all humanity
Becomes as the Divine Child—
Pure, holy, creative and innocent.

That we overcome this world of illusion,
That we be reborn and readied
Through the Blessed Mother's Love.
That we inherit the Kingdom of Heaven
Upon this hallowed Earth.

AUM (All United in Mary) (3x)

Beloved Lord Mary,
Mother of the Cosmic Christ

Mary Clarice McChrist

19. The third decant (Recite 5 -10x). Group may recite (1x or 3x).

The Rosary for the Inner Child

Hail Mary, Mother of the Immaculate Infant,
Watch with me, heal my inner child.
Transmute my birth, all pain, and denial.
I Am reborn with innocence and childlike Purity.

Hail Mary, Mother of the Immaculate Infant,
May I behold the world with curious eyes,
May I touch the flowers and hear the songbirds.
Help me to express Joy and Love to all beings.

Hail Mary, Mother of the Immaculate Infant,
May I become Centered and Still within,
Knowing You direct and guide my Path,
Mary, my Mother, rock me upon your knee.

Beloved Lord Mary,
Queen of Peace

Mary Clarice McChrist

Our lady of the Rose
by Enrico Rello, Turin

The Black Madonna
by Mary Sylvia McChrist

20. Recite on large bead following the third decant.

Prayer for the Transmutation of World Sorrow

O Sacred Black Madonna,
O Holy Mother of God,
Draw from myself
And this beloved planet,
All pain, sorrow, and disease.
May the Divine Feminine in humanity
Be honored throughout the world.

Transmute the great Tribulation
Of Earth shifts and changes,
That the Blessed Mother Earth
Beneath our feet
Might be freed from
The crushing weight of illusion
Created through people's own ignorance.

AUM (All United in Mary) (3x)

The Black Madonna
Mary Clarice McChrist

*The Black Madonna /Mary Magdalene
Apparition from Italy, Photographer Unknown*

21. *The fourth decant (Recite (5 - 10x). Group may recite (1x 3x)*

The Black Madonna Rosary

Black Madonna, Mother of the Void,
Blessed art Thou, transmuter of sorrow.
Blessed art Thou, Mary Magdalene,
Lady of Our Lord, Jesus the Christ.

Hail Mary, Magdalene of Love,
Open my heart,
Through thy Path of Tears.

Mary Magdalene

Mary Clarice McChrist

22. Recite 3x at the end of the fourth decant.

Prayer for Holding the Immaculate Concept

O Glorious Rainbow Lady,
Holy Lord Mary Buddha, my Mother,
Help me to hold the Immaculate Concept
Of perfect man, woman, and child,
Of a New Heaven and a New Earth—
As we transcend the old Piscean order
And, like the jeweled phoenix bird,
Ascend into a World of Divine Order.

O Glorious Rainbow Lady,
Open my being to God's perfect healing.
O Mother of Many Colors,
May I align with your Divine Nature.
Prepare my body for Divine Union*
With my Beloved I Am Self
That I may always embody
My Immaculate Concept of Being.

AUM (All United in Mary) (3x)

Lord Mary Buddha

Mary Clarice McChrist

---

* *Complete Union of the I Am Presence would create the 5th-12th dimensional body, aligned with all 12 strands of DNA. This is the body of the New Heaven.*

Lord Mary Buddha
by Mary Sylvia McChrist

23. *The fifth decant (Recite 9 x). Group may recite (1x or 2x).*

The Blessed Ascension Rosary

Hail Mary, full of Grace,
The Lord is with Thee.
Blessed art Thou among women, and
Blessed is the Fruit of Thy Womb, Jesus.

Holy Mary, Mother of us all,
Blend with us, children of the Sun (Son),
For we have consciously won our ascension,
Right now and forevermore, I AM!

Conclusion of the rosary; last bead

Hail Mary, full of Grace,
The Lord is with Thee.
Blessed art Thou among women, and
Blessed is the Fruit of Thy Womb, Jesus.

Beloved, Sweet Mary, Mother of us all,
I surrender my heart and give devotion to Thee,
That Thou shall release my burdens,
And reveal unto me that which I must do
To heal my pain and the suffering of others.

Beloved Lord Mary,
Mother of the Cosmic Christ

Mary Clarice McChrist

24. Recite on the Heart Medal following fifth decant.
   Feel the clockwise momentum of the Mother's Love.

I Am Your Mother

I Am your Mother: all people,
All races, all creeds, all religions.
I Am your Mother, all people.
Come now and sit upon My Knee.
Come now unto My Arms and rest.

For the Mother frees you *now*
Through the Power of Divine Love,
The Feminine Principle of all life.
Our Mother-Father God is All.

God is both Infinite Power
And Infinite Love and Wisdom.
What She/He is, you are also.
As we are One with God,
All that God is, we are!

I Am Lord Mary,
Mother of the Cosmic Christ

Lord of Lords

Mary Clarice McChrist

25. Hold your Rosary Beads. Charge them with your Love and Light.

Increasing the Rosary Momentum

Beloved Lord Mary,
Mother of the Cosmic Christ,
I ask that You increase the radiance
Of my Rosary Prayer
By the Power of the 10 trillion X 10 trillion
With full God-Goddess Power.

I also request that my angels, my child-self,
Christ Self, and Mother-Father Self
Continue the momentum
Of *The Blessed Ascension Rosary*
Throughout the day and night.

I Am Lord Mary,
Mother of the Cosmic Christ

Lord of Lords

Mary Clarice McChrist

26. Gather the Rosary Beads into your hand.

☦

The Sign of the Cross

In the Name of the Father,
(Touch Rosary to 3rd eye center/forehead.)

The Mother,
(Touch your heart center/mid-chest.)

The Daughter and the Son,
(Touch left of heart.)

And the Holy Soul/Holy Spirit,
(Touch your right side opposite your heart.)

It is so done! (3x)
(Touch your heart center.)

Amen, Ah-women, Ah-child, All One.

I Am Lord Mary,
Mother of the Cosmic Christ

Mary Clarice McChrist

27. Completion and blessing of yourself and your beads.

Closing Prayer

Let the Three-Fold Blessing of
The Mother, the Father,
The Daughter/Son,
Be multiplied in your Joyful Heart
Forevermore, I AM!

May the Holy Soul/Holy Spirit,
The symbolic Dove,
Give you wings to transcend
All less than the purest Cosmic Christ Truth.

For Beloved, I Am your Mother,

Your Comforter, worlds without end.

AUM (All United in Mary) (3x)

Mary Clarice McChrist

Madonna and Child
by William Adolph Bouguereau 1825-1905

28. Recite in unison thus completing your daily Rosary Prayers.

Cosmic Mother's Sealing Prayer

In the Name and by the Power of Myself as Cosmic Mother, I invoke the complete healing of all dimensions, of all time/space framesl of all realities: *lokas* (physical, subtle, and causal worlds); all *gunas* (universal qualities of harmony, agitation, and inertia); and all *kalas*, (past, present, and future). May all be restored to perfection and bliss.

So be it! It is so done!

May all waters be purified, all blood healed and restored to the Starfire Presence of the Mother. May all hearts be healed, all souls be safe and protected by Archangel Michael and His Bands of Angels. May all sense of separation vanish, and relationships meet, all human and divine requirements. May despair be gone, the voices of the children be raised in song, and the old ones laugh at the Cosmic Joke of Life.

So be it!

Mary Clarice McChrist

Blue Rose Prayers • *119*

29. Play or sing *Ave Maria*.

Ave Maria

A-ve Ma-ri - - a! gra-ti-a - - ple—na,
Ma-ri-a, gra—ti-a ple-na, Ma-ri-a, gra—ti-a - ple-na.
A-ve, A-ve! Do-mi-nus, do-mi-nus te-cum,
Be-ne-dic-ta tu in mu-li-e-ri-bus,
Et be-ne-di-ctus, fruc-tus ven-tri tu-i, Je-sus.

A- - - ve Ma- ri- - -a! A-ve Ma-ri- -a!
Ma-ter De-i, O-ra pro no-bis pec-ca-to-ri-bus,
O-ra, o-ra pro no-bis,
O-ra, o-ra pro no-bis pec-ca-to-ri-bus,

Nunc et in ho-ra - - mor-tis,
In ho-ra mor-tis nos-trae,
In ho-ra mor-tis, mor- -tis nos-trae,
In ho-ra mor-tis no- - strae.

A - ve Ma-ri- - a! A - ve Ma-ri - - a!
Gra-ti-a ple- -na. Ma-ri-a,
Gra- -ti-a- - ple-na,
Ma-ri - a, gra - - ti-a- - ple-na.

A - ve, A - ve! Do-mi-nus, Do-mi-nus te cum;
Be-ne-dic - - - tus,
Et be-ne-dic-tus fruc-tus ven-tris tu-i, Je- - sus.
A - ve Ma-ri - - a!

30. Sing song or use CD
Words: Mary Clarice McChrist Melody: Original

I Am Presence Song

I Am Presence ever near me,
Come be with me everyday.
My great Love, Honor and Glory,
Floods to you all through the day.

Fill me with, all Thou art,
Love, abundance, flows to me.
Test me truly, I Am Worthy,
I'm a Flaming Light
In your Rainbow Sea.

I Am Presence, all I do
Floods unto me from You.
You're my God-Star,
A shining Sun.
O Beloved, are we now One.

I Am Presence ever near me,
Come be with me everyday.
My great Love, Honor and Glory
Floods to you all through the day.

31. Receive a transmission from Lord Mary or play a tape of one of Her dictations through Mary Clarice McChrist available from: www.mother-matrix.org.
32. Read *Lord Mary's Request* for the group closing.

Lord Mary's Request

"I ask that you continue to give The Blessed Ascension Rosary daily, as it is the most powerful prayer yet released for the transmutation of world sorrow and for your own God-Divinity and personal ascension. These prayers directly promote the Ascension of Earth.

"I cannot emphasize this enough, <u>for you are saving souls with your prayers.</u> *If you saw the future as I have, or the now being experienced by many of my children, you would never for one second consider not doing your Blue Rose Prayers.*

"The Hours of Mercy are soon to be over. Anti-evolutionary energies will no longer be tolerated. Do your part. Create a positive prayer momentum with your prayers. Beloved Ones, making *The Blessed Ascension Rosary* part of your daily ritual is the wisest decision of all!"

I Am Lord Mary,
Queen of Heaven and Co-Redeemer With Christ

Mary Clarice McChrist

33. Read *Mary's Rose Crusade*.

Mary's Rose Crusade for World Peace

Beloved children of the Sun (Son),

My Blessing permeates your being and world. Help us cover the map of the world with roses. Each time a new group forms, I ask that the group leader write, phone, or e-mail Mary Clarice and ask that your group be indicated with a *blue rose* on the Peace Map. In this manner, many New Crusaders for Peace will be encouraged to join in our project. Please also send to Mary Clarice the names and addresses of individuals who commit to the daily recitation of the Blue Rose Prayers. These names will be placed on our mailing list and protected in confidence.

Dearly beloved, we are changing prophecy and anchoring Heaven on Earth. A *white rose* will be shown on the map for each person who daily recites *The Blessed Ascension Rosary* or *The Rosary of Tribulation*. May the map be covered with roses of the Mother as we transform the world into a breathtaking bouquet of roses.

I Am Your Mother, Lord Mary, Queen of Peace

Mary Clarice McChrist
The Mother Matrix
P. O. Box 1178, Mt. Shasta, CA 96067
E-mail: mary-ma@mother-matrix.org

Chapter 7

Blue Rose World Service Groups

The Purpose of the Blue Rose Groups

Divine Mother's Purpose for each Group:

1. To spread *The Blessed Ascension Rosary* prayer and *The Rosary of Tribulation* prayer across the planet.

2. To share the Love of Divine Mother Mary with all of Her children.

3. To form world service prayer groups whose weekly prayer momentum can be counted on by Spirit.

4. To create supportive spiritual families of like-hearted individuals who can be called upon to help transmute energies during emergency situations.

5. To come together for the purpose of healing each other and our beloved planet.

6. To bring forth the direct teachings of Divine Mother Mary and Beloved Lord Jesus through books, visionary art, tapes, CDs, and the Mother Matrix Web Site.

7. To network Mary Clarice McChrist's events and to support Marian group leaders in their missions of service to the Light.

Blue Rose World Service Groups

The Blessed Mother's *Blue Rose World Service Groups* began forming when the initial prayers were first released in 1991. As your personal devotion grows, you may also wish to join with others to pray. "Where two or more are gathered in My Name, there Am I." Christ emphasized the importance of group prayer. Each person multiplies the momentum of the prayers by the power of square: the number of people praying times the number of people praying.

It is for this reason that I ask you to consider forming a *Blue Rose World Service Prayer Group*. Talk to me; let us pray together. Timing is important. Become a group leader only if you feel called by Me to do so.

Even if you do not feel you should lead a group at this time, you could be instrumental in sharing this book with your spiritual friends. Has this work helped you? Are you and your relationships improving? Do you feel My Presence? Perhaps your testimony will encourage and strengthen others.

I Am Lord Mary,
Queen of Peace

Mary Clarice McChrist

My Ambassadors of Peace

Dear Blue Rose World Service Groups,

Each group leader is a special ambassador of Myself, Mother Mary. I Am with you, helping you create the perfect environment for your *Blue Rose World Service Group*. Be aware of My Presence. Listen to your Mother. I place each group participant under My Grace.

I have been so pleased with your responses to My Heart's Call. Dear Ones, come to your Mother. We must wrap our Love around the planet. I would be so pleased for individuals in the *Blue Rose World Service Groups* to begin networking with each other through e-mail, letters, or phone calls. Keep in direct contact with Mary Clarice as she is the coordinator of the Mother Matrix World Network. This Mother Matrix of Divine Love is flowing in, under, and through the planetary Christ Grid. It is strengthening and healing our planet. You are initiating a powerful group focus which is not to be underestimated.

How exciting it is to know more and more groups will be created as Mother's Love directly touches each child of God. Let us know the names, addresses, phone, e-mail address, and web sites of anyone in your group. Also, indicate if the person is willing to dedicate themselves to say the prayers on a daily basis.

As mentioned, we will have a world map on our site which will use *blue roses* to indicate Rosary

Groups who are reciting daily Blue Rose Prayers and *white roses* to indicate the individuals who are reciting prayers. It will be fun to watch the map light up.

I ask each of you to network for your own group and the Mother Matrix Web Site: www.mother-matrix.org. Share the messages, prayers, and testimonies posted on our site. Print them off and use some at your meetings. Help draw in others who you feel would benefit from the personal healing and group support generated within our precious groups of Light. *I Am multiplying Myself through each one of you.* Please do protection prayers for each other during this Time of Tribulation.

Your testimonies and experiences are beginning to flow into the Mother Matrix web site. Please send in your comments, as these inspire others to pray *The Blessed Ascension Rosary* daily or to create their own *Blue Rose World Service Group.*

I Am Your Delighted Mother,
Queen of Peace

Mary Clarice McChrist

Creating Your Blue Rose Event

Preparing Your Sanctuary

Everything affects everything else. The falling of one leaf affects the entire forest.

All is energy and thought. Each person who enters a room affects the whole atmosphere. Their aura, thoughts, vibration, words and actions impact the environment.

Why build this temple space in your own home?

Do you remember the words from the film *Field of Dreams*? "If you build it, they will come." The higher planes easily interface with the Earth at this time. If we prepare a place in our consciousness and our home, higher energies come to be with us.

You can create an intention for a room and consciously build its vibration into a Sanctuary of Peace and Divine Harmony. Without such an intention, the highest vibrations are rarely achieved. Because it is your space, you have the right to maintain it as you wish.

Simplicity is best for some people. It depends on your soul ray and your temperament.

Holy photos, artwork, statues, crystals, and fountains are all reminders of Spirit that help people realize they have entered a Sacred Space. Meditate in your temple room. Ask your Higher Self and your Council of Light—your etheric master teachers and guides—to communicate with you and show you what color and quality would be most auspicious for your particular room.

With what energies do you feel most aligned? Are you most comfortable with Mary and Christ, the Buddha, a particular Divine Mother or saint or Hindu deity? This is your environment. It is a reflection of you, your spiritual feelings and alignment. There is no judgment on any choice you make, including not creating a holy space. All is One.

Aligning Your Home

Alignment Decree:

"Divine Mother Matrix, align my home, this Temple of the Divine Mother, with its highest Divine purpose." (3x)

You could ask that only those of like-mind enter your space. You can anchor a Vortex of Violet Flame outside your front door in order to transmute all incoming energies.

Anchoring the Violet Flame

"In the Name and by the Power of Saint Germain and Portia, I call forth a Violet Flame Vortex and anchor it here right now with full God-Power." (3x)

Use your hands to pull down the Violet Flame from the Inner Planes. Anchor a flame outside and another flame inside your front door. You may wish to anchor it elsewhere as well.

"I call this Violet Flame to transmute everyone and everything that enters my holy space.

"I call this Conscious Singing Flame of St. Germain to be ever sustained and increased with this decree."

Invite all of your spiritual guests to stand in the Violet Flame as they enter. When the person is cleared, his or her aura will become golden, which enlivens the mental consciousness of the mind and each cell of the physical being.

Calling Forth the Cities of Light

The Ascended Masters have prophesied twelve cities of Light. Where there are twelve, the thirteenth is usually hidden. These cities are already etherically present in the atmosphere. They carry tremendous energies of Divine Will and Presence. The primary cities of Light shall be completely lowered into the 5th-7th dimensional field of Earth by 2005. These cities are presently hovering in the etheric levels above the following locations:

1. Mt. Shasta, California, USA, the first city of Light.
2. State of Washington, USA, cycling over the areas of Mt. Adams, Mt. Rainier, and Mt. Olympia.
3. Near Mt. Meru, Peru.
4. Falconwing, Colorado, USA.

5. Near Stockholm, Sweden.
6. Near Beijing, China.
7. Dornburg, Thalheim, Germany, near Mother Meera's Ashram.
8. Near Longreach, Queensland, Australia.
9. Virginia, USA, between Lynchburg and Richmond.
10. Southeast Alaska, USA, near the Canadian border.
11. Mt. Popocatépetl, near Mexico City, Mexico.
12. Near Lake Simcoe, Ontario, Canada.
13. Pondicherry, India, above the Ashram of Sri Aurobindo and Sweet Mother (Mira Richard).

These cities may not remain exactly as stated, due to Earth changes or unforeseen events. However, key people are already being magnetized into these areas to anchor their Light. Please forward any information you have on these areas.

By calling for the anchoring of the Holy Pillars, you are aligning with this awesome activity.

"I call forth the Pillars of the City of Light of Mt. Shasta to anchor in the corners of this room/temple in (put in your location)."

You may also wish to call in the Pillars for other locations.

The Altar Focus

The temple room often requires an altar, a focus for spiritual practice. The altar is the symbolic Spirit. It represents air, earth, fire, water, and ether. Create a space which is holy to you.

The air element, the presence and absence of shapes and objects, all set a tone.

Earth may be represented by wood, a statue, crystals, pebbles or flowers.

Fire cleanses and clears the space. Candles may be in various rainbow colors to represent the Rays of God. Pictorial religious candles carry the Power of the One they illustrate.

Water can be represented by a small fountain or a goblet which is symbolic of the Holy Grail.

Ether is itself, and doesn't need a symbol.

Creating an altar can be an act of deep meditation. Allow your God-Self to direct you. What objects and symbols are appropriate to you? Where should they be placed? Flow without thought. The heart can feel the perfection as it manifests. You will be directed in every action.

Dedicate your altar as you wish, in accordance with your heart's desire.

Dedication for Blue Rose World Service Work

I call on Beloved Lord Mary. (3x)

Please anchor rays of intense Love and Light which shall blaze forth from this temple.

Blessed Mother, I dedicate this temple to You and to Your Immaculate Sacred Heart.

Please purify me, instruct me, and allow me to reach my full spiritual and human potential. I honor You as my Divine Mother. May I become Your Perfect Child of Peace.

Anchoring the Light

Your temple room has been dedicated; your intention is set. The altar has been created.

The Violet Flame has been established outside and inside your front door and other places that you feel are appropriate.

Pillars of Light are anchored in the four corners of the temple space.

Now you are ready for your first gathering, or better still, *to initiate the space with your own prayers and meditation.* Use the prayers in this book to begin building the energy-field in your home.

The Power of Music

Music is more than ambiance. It is creative power. Music should match your intention. Music sets the field. What chakra centers are most appropriate for your work? Are you doing prayers, healings, or ceremony? What is the effect of the music? How does it enhance or detract from the program you wish to present? Live music is best, but many incredible pieces are available on CD or cassette.

Open the program with a high-vibration piece. Perhaps the words indicate the subject you are exploring. Collect music that touches you deeply.

Group chanting with live music or to a recording can be very effective. Your cellular consciousness can eventually resonate with a living mantra. It can become the song of the cells as Sweet Mother proved with Her Twin Ray, Sri Aurobindo, in Pondicherry, India. Explore the use of one or more mantras. *The Blessed Ascension Rosary* also works in a similar manner within your cells. Your whole being may hum the Rosary.

Refer to the Music Appendix on page 221 for several musical selections.

The Double Dorje

The Double Dorje is a power symbol in Buddhism and assists in the harmonizing of East and West. Grounding into the Double Dorje is an important step in the Blue Rose World Service Ritual.

A symbolic Double Dorje, represented by a Lotus and a Rose at the center of the Earth was anchored in Mother Earth on December 19, 1999, and activated on the Winter Solstice, December 21, 1999, from the Temple of the Mother in Dunsmuir, California.

This represented the anchoring of the Godhead upon and within Mother Earth. There was also a transfer of Power from the Father to the Mother at this time.

The Lotus, representing the vertical arm of the dorje, is held by Lord Buddha (North) and Lord Mary Buddha (South). The Rose, representing the horizontal arm, is held by Lord Mary (West) and Lord Jesus (East).

Each human on Earth who has chosen to align with God now carries this as a miniature field of Love within their heart.

As the New Year's bells tolled on December 31, 1999, there was an activation of this Double Dorje which swept across the Earth. The waves of Divine Love and Bliss released were absolutely incredible, causing spontaneous tears in myself and those around me. We were in gratitude.

Blue Rose World Service Group Format

(Each group is unique)

7 - 7:30 PM

Pass through the Violet Flame.

Remove shoes.

Each person may be cleared using sage or a bell. A bell or sage is moved in front of each chakra and down the person's back to clear the auric field.

Every person signs in: name, address, phone, and e-mail. The phone number is required to call people for the next gathering.

Tea is appreciated by many. Bonding with the group is recommended.

Energy exchange is important. Help should be given to prepare the sanctuary and clean up following the meeting. One person is not to do everything. A donation is often appropriate. This depends on the circumstances of the people involved in your group.

7:30 PM The Blue Rose Group begins on time.

1. Opening music or song. See Music Appendix on page 221 for suggestions.

2. Bring forth the Archangels and Divine Emissaries:

   I call the great Cosmic Archangels to descend with their Twins.

   Gabriel and Hope, Archangels of the White Ray, hold the North Pillar.

   Jophiel and Christine, Archangels of the Yellow Ray, hold the East Pillar.

   Chamuel and Charity, Archangels of the Pink Ray, hold the South Pillar.

   Michael and Faith, Archangels of the Blue Ray, hold the West Pillar.

   Raphael and Lady Regina, Archangels of the Green Ray, hold Healing Light in the Center of our circle.

   Lord Mary anchors the Heart of Divine Mother above the Center of our Matrix.

   Sandalphon connects us deeply with the Earth below the center of our circle.

   Lord Metatron brings forth a Canopy of Living Light about us from the Heavens.

   We call that each person be gently adjusted to the vibration of the room by his or her Higher Self. I invoke Divine Harmony, Clarity, Love, and Peace right now with full God-Power. May each person's field and purpose be clarified and strengthened.

Collectively, we work in Harmony with Love, Integrity, and Divine Purpose. So be it!

3. Opening prayer by the group leader.
4. Call in the Saints, Sages, Ascended Masters, Elohim, and Divine Mothers-Fathers. Each person feels free to call in the Beings one after another.

I call forth...

Grounding the Energy and the Intention

5. Stand in a circle holding hands. Group leader reads aloud:

Connect with each person through the heart. Send love to the person on your right and allow the love to circulate all the way around until it returns to you.

We ask that the energy be grounded through our feet into the center of Mother Earth.

Send a column of Light, down from your hips and base chakra at the bottom of your spine into the core of Mother Earth.

Connect with the Double Dorje in the center of Earth. Remember the vertical arm of the Dorje is held by Lord Buddha (N) and Lord Mary Buddha (S), and the horizontal arm is held by Lord Mary (W) and Lord Jesus (E).

We now connect with these Beings and draw this energy and that of Mother Gaia up through our bodies, anchoring us firmly into Terra.

Let us anchor this intention with three OMs.

6. Call forth aloud regarding any people or events you feel require healing energy.
7. Continue with Chapter 5 *World Service Devotions*, and Chapter 6 *The Blue Rose Prayers*.

Group Leaders

The group leader is representing Divinity in form. She or he should embody Compassion, Love, Wisdom, and Power. The leader establishes the energy field info the room and is responsible for "holding the energy field" and continuing the prayer momentum in the absence of the group.

Another peer might be assigned to phone the group and remind them of the upcoming Blue Rose Gathering. <u>Please contact Mary Clarice so that your group can be placed on the web site listing of groups throughout the world.</u>

It is recommended that the meetings be on Thursday evenings from 7 to 9:30 PM. This is a sacred day to Mother Mary. Sunday, during the day or evening, is a good alternative time. Having the group arrive at 7:00 PM for socializing and tea is desirable. Refreshments may or may not be served. This should be a shared responsibility. A donation should be arrangedto cover flyers, tea and candles in order not to burden the host or hostess.

People are required to be present and settled by the

time the program is scheduled to start at exactly at 7:30 PM. Spirit will be present and is not to be kept waiting.

The core group should be committed to Spirit. **Your prayers are important. Spirit depends on these Blue Rose groups to serve humanity.** Discuss this with your group.

Send testimonials of healings and special experiences with the Mother, angels, or the group itself to the Mother Matrix in California. These serve to inspire other potential Blue Rose gatherings. Also, share problems or group requirements.

Even though suggestions are presented here, each Blue Rose Group is unique. All gatherings will be different, even if a similar format is utilized. Spirit directs the gatherings, expanding and weaving the group energies and dynamics together to meet the intention for the evening. Often world or local events or group member requirements for healing will present themselves.

The most important qualities to be present at all *Blue Rose World Service Group* meetings are: open hearts, the presence of Love in the space, and openness, friendship and bonding among the souls present. Each person comes as called by the Divine Mother or the Master within.

Soul families are drawn together and honor each other. Occasionally, a person may not resonate with the Rosary work; this is fine. No judgment is to be expressed.

Occasionally, a former Catholic person will not be able to recite *The Blessed Ascension Rosary* because of painful past experiences. It is fine for some people to sit in silence while others recite the prayers. Free will is very precious and is not to be interfered with. As people move in and out of the *Blue Rose Groups,* bless them and be at Peace. All is well. There is no judgment.

Group Initiations

Ascension and other Initiations will be given in these groups for individuals and all group participants. *When the disciples are ready, the Master arrives.* This Master Presence may be within or without. When the students are ready, the next steps will be available. When the group is ready, an Initiation will be given. If a messenger or channel is the leader, this is especially convenient for direction to be given by Mother Mary, Jesus, or another Master Presence.

Spirit can come through and direct the group ritual. *Take special note of events in which unusually high energy is felt and the group is raised into the next level of perfection.* Ask and record what Initiations are given.

What is a Messenger?

A messenger is trained by an Ascended Master to bring forth the Words, Energy Field, and Essence of Spirit. *A channel merely relays the words.* There is not a major transference of energy to the audience with a channel. Both messenger and channel should have gone through rigorous personal training to purify and perfect their physical instrument and the purity of the communication.

A full-body conscious channel of the Ascended

Masters is a step below a messenger. Full-body means that Spirit is fully animating the physical body from head to toe. Conscious means one is fully aware of what is transpiring. A medium, in contrast, is out of the body and does not recall what has been said when the communication is complete. The Ascended Masters disapprove of this method, as it can be dangerous for the physical vehicle.

Mary Clarice has worked as a messenger for many years. If a messenger or trusted channel has been assigned by Lord Mary to work with your group, this is a special blessing. However, if you feel the information coming to your group is incorrect, or some problems arise with the communication, please contact the Mother Matrix, as each group is a reflection of Mother Mary, and the highest standards are to be maintained.

Human ego should be practically nonexistent in the group leader. Problems should be addressed and worked on by group members. If not resolved, they should be addressed by the whole group. This is sometimes part of the preparation and healing that goes on prior to a group Initiation. Not all groups resolve their problems and take the Initiation into the next level of attainment.

Finesse is a requirement. *Divine Love can melt all human problems.* Being willing to heal that which is in yourself as it is being mirrored to you by others is a valuable lesson. Feel the Blessing of Divine Mother.

Mary, Queen of Peace

Discrimination: Testing the Spirit

1. Can you discriminate? When Spirit comes to you, test it. Ask three three times, "Are you of the highest purest Christ Light?" Anti-evolutionary beings can lie twice, but the third time, they must respond with Truth. At this point they might just disappear, or you may call Archangel Michael for help.

   "Archangel Michael come forth now! (3x) This being requires your escort into the Light. Please do this now!"

   You can also call the Indian Runner Angels or In God We Trust Angels to assist Archangel Michael in this process. Lord Metatron may be called on for difficult cases.

2. You are tested on each level of the Path. Be wise. <u>Just because someone is out-of-body does not make them an Ascended Master or Archangel of the Light.</u>

3. Engage your heart. Is there Truth in what this being is saying clairaudiently, with an actual voice which may be inside or outside yourself, or through mental telepathy, in which you are receiving a transference of actual thought? How do you feel? Are you fearful or do you feel uplifted?

4. Muscle testing can be accurate for some people. Instead of doing full arm kinesiology, use your fingers. Form a circle with your thumb and index finger. Do the same with your other hand.

Link the circles together and pull apart slightly. Tell your etheric Council of Light (your Teachers and guides) that if the answer is *yes*, then the fingers are to remain closed. If the answer is *no*, then the fingers will pull apart spontaneously.

Ask: "Am I ____ (your name)?" Then ask several yes-or-no questions. Get this established with the personal Council of Light that works with you.

5. Set up a system with your etheric Teachers and guides. Ask to feel a throb or pulse within your heart center when something is true. This same pulse will be felt in your solar plexus if the information or being is false. Work with this technique.

6. Intuition may be your best guide. What do you feel intuitively? Does your heart agree? <u>A pendulum may be used also, but be careful that this does not become a crutch</u>. Some people become completely dependent upon their pendulums. Move to a higher form of knowing as soon as possible (see #5).

7. Most high beings have one or more Ascended Masters assigned to them. This is a very Sacred Relationship. You eventually know and trust the Ascended Masters who work with you. You will immediately be able to identify their vibration as they approach your aura. A good rule of thumb is to stick with known teachers such as Mary and Jesus. They also must be tested, for there are many imposters.

8. When you absolutely know an energetic imprint, ask that Ascended Master teacher to come forth and identify any new communicators. *The testing of your discrimination never stops.* Better to be wise and cautious than to be sorry.

9. Often you will be assigned to one Master and then moved on to another. You may be set-up to see how you do and how well you can handle problems. *Your ego will be tested repeatedly.*

10. Confusion also occurs because of multiple Earths and versions of time. A being could be the Christ of Arcturus and yet not be the Christ Jesus on this Earth. A being might be Lord Jesus of this Earth, a Sananda-Christ* from another galaxy, or an imposter from the astral planes who is attempting to deceive you. Can you tell the difference? The Father says, "Test them before you trust them."

11. The seasoning of a messenger or channel takes years. Your percentage of accuracy increases as the dimensional level, from which you receive, rises. Your accuracy should be from 95--100%, and you should be receiving from the sixth dimension or higher before you start teaching or influencing others with your words. Otherwise, you may be misguiding others.

---

* See "Sananda" in *Glossary of Divone Beings on page 231.*

*Apparition of Lord Michael
by Unknown Photographer*

Chapter 8

Winning the Protection Game

Winning the Protection Game

Dearly Beloved Ones,

On the 3rd and 4th dimension, protection is required. This is because duality is present and active as polarity. As you shift from the earthly self to a Divine Light Being, anti-evolutionary energies test your strength.

Every time that you move up in your Initiation, you are tested to see <u>if you can hold your new level of energy</u>, or whether you will fall into mistrust, anger, and despair.

It is perhaps best to think of this as a game of duality, like a chess game. Often, beings or circumstances that come to test you have permission of the Light to do so.

Archangel Michael

There are tools required to play this game. You may call on help from the Inner Planes:

First of all, Archangel Michael and the Legions of Light and Power are assigned to aid humanity. Call for Archangel Michael three times (3x). Indian Runner Angels (the same as Native American Angels), and the In God We Trust Angels, are all part of His Team.

"Archangel Michael (3x), come forth, NOW! I Am having trouble... (Explain the circumstances you need help with.) Please clear and assist me with this problem."

The Sword of Michael

Archangel Michael carries an etheric Sword of dazzling blue lightning. As He wields this Sword, the Light of 10,000 Suns cuts through all darkness.

As you and Michael work together and you pass your Initiations, Michael will give you an etheric replica of His Sword. You may certainly ask Him for your Sword, and it will be presented to you when the time is right.

Recite the *Lord Michael Decree*:

"Beloved Archangel Michael (3x), please give me my Sword of Truth."(3x)

(Hold out your dominant hand and wait.)

If this is your Divine Moment for this Initiation, Archangel Michael will place the Sword in your hand. Even if you cannot see it, you will feel the weight of it in your hand.

Our sincere thanks to our blessed brother and friend, Archangel Michael, called Christ Michael by some beings. Lord Michael is Archangel Michael's Higher Aspect. He is the Creator of our universe.

Our deep appreciation to them both!

I Am Lord Mary,
Mother of All People
Mary Clarice McChrist

Archangel Michael Speaks

Warriors of the Light,

You will still be tested, as you must learn experientially how to hold your auric field and your psychic space in your home, car, environment, and work space.

The Sword is used to cut you free from unwanted energies, or forces wishing to distract you from your ever-present connection with the flow, Mother-Father God.

Of course, all these anti-evolutionary energies are illusion, but on the 3rd and 4th dimensions they appear very real.

As moths are attracted to light, your Light attracts darkness. This is not to be feared.

You are never given a test too difficult for you to handle. Call for help. This is part of the game. Learn your lessons. Be vigilant in your clearing routine, and realize that I Am always ready to assist you.

"But, Michael, how can you be everywhere at once?" you might ask. There is no time and space. I Am One with everything. Therefore, I Am always available to you.

The Noble Sword of Michael

Feel the weight of My Sword in your hand. Your Sword is an exact replica of Mine, except that it is designed for you. To give you a Sword beyond your attainment would not be a kindness to you.

An example of My great Sword is Excalibur, King Arthur's Sword. King Arthur's Excalibur was My <u>True Sword</u>. It had full potency, but even Arthur, one of My Bodies, could not hold the Purity of its Power for long. To do that, he would have had to give Guinevere to Lancelot, for they were Twin Flames. Furthermore, he would have had to serve shoulder to shoulder with both of them. This type of Wisdom, Srength, and Compassion would have allowed him to serve both Christ and the Goddess equally. The kingdom would have shifted to the 5th dimension, beyond duality, and a Golden Age would have manifested.

King Arthur did not really fail. He was a great man who served as an archetype for humanity. Arthur returns through each person who overcomes his own ego self and who rises beyond the human to serve only Divine Will. Thus one knows complete surrender, not to the enemy, but to his or her Divine God Presence. Only then can one serve the Highest Cause.

Using Your Sword of Truth

Children, particularly the Indigo children, are sharing with humanity *the power of pretending.* By pretending, you are manifesting images and thoughts on the subtle planes. Pretend that your Sword is real. It really is. Store it etherically in a sheath by your side. It is immediately ready for any action you desire.

Your Sword of Truth may be used in several ways:

1. Cut your crown chakra free each morning. Trace around body, arms, torso, legs, and feet. Trace your whole outline with the Sword. This clears away unwanted or stale energies, cleaning your aura for the new day.
2. You can hold your Sword and move it in a circle. "In the Name of Archangel Michael, I clear this space." You can go through each room and purify the space.
3. Drawing the Sword in an infinity symbol, the Cosmic Eight, is also powerful. You can clear a room and then bring in a vortex with the Cosmic Eight.
4. Chakras may be cleared with the infinity symbol. To draw the Cosmic Eight, use your Sword over each chakra that you intend to clear. Also, clear 8-12 above your head.
5. When you are done, ask, "Are all of my chakras cleared?" Get the answer internally, use a pendulum, or finger muscle test. (See Glossary of Terms on page 232.)

Are You Corded?

The term 'cording' refers to an etheric connection between your chakras and other beings. Much energy may be lost in this manner. Cording may be a form of controlling you, and it is not recommended by the Masters. Some earthly teachers purposely cord their students, which is very unethical.

Are any of your chakras corded? You may wish to check chakras 1 thru 7, 8 thru 12, and higher. If you are corded, call on me, Archangel Michael, to come forth and remove the cords. You may learn to gently pull out the cord, release its tiny roots, and send it back to the sender with forgiveness and your firm intention that no more cording is to occur.

A mother and very young child—birth to 3 years of age—or a sickly child, may be corded together to strengthen the child. Ask Mother Mary if it is appropriate in your individual case.

Most people who are corded together do not cord consciously with another person. They merely think of the partner or child, and the cord forms. Cords can cause you to feel weak and tired. Ask yourself in that instance, "Am I corded?" If so, clear it immediately. I Am always ready to assist you in any cases related to protection.

I Am Lord Michael
Mary Clarice McChrist

My Sovereignty Prayer

Great Supreme Mother,
Mother-Father of Love,

I make the call to come under your Absolute Protection right now with full God-Power.

I call forgiveness for any transgression or action against the Divine Plan which I may have made knowingly or unknowingly. I seek Absolute Sovereignty of my human form: my sexual organs, my emotions, my heart, my mind, and my auric field. This protection is eternally sustained both day and night by Archangel Michael's Program #1. I call for all dimensions and levels of myself to be Protected, Purified, and Enlightened in accordance with the Will of the Supreme Mother and the Father-Mother of Absolute Love.

Let the gapped energy, the twist, the distortion, and chaos of the lower gods and creation have no effect on me, my life, my mission, my karma or family.

I call to be lifted above all energies of separation and duality, and to heal myself and my experiences. I ask to be gently purified and aligned with Jesus, the Cosmic Christ, and His Mother, Lord Mary. I ask to be taken to Mary's Retreat each night to receive healing, instruction, and clarity on all incidents.

I call to encode all my learnings at a cellular level. I Am freed of all plagues, dis-ease or pestilence. I ask to shift into my highest Truth and the vibration which is appropriate for me at the time.

I call that my unhealed Life Lessons be healed and purified in the Heart Flame of the Mother, Lord Mary, and Her Son, Jesus!

I ask that everything called for here be the highest Truth, and be adjusted, if necessary, by my Higher Self. I call to be Resurrected, aligned, and under the Supreme Mother and the Father of the Highest Love.

That which I call for myself, I ask also for my family, both personal and spiritual, and for all women, men, and children upon Mother Earth.

So Be It!

Beloved I Am! (3x)

Thank You, Supreme Mother.
Thank You, Great God of Love.
Thank You, Lord Jesus and the Mother, Lord Mary!

Mary Clarice McChrist

The Rainbow Protection of Archangel Michael

Archangel Michael! (3x)

1. Archangel Michael, place a Conscious Sphere of Blue Lighting about me now!
2. Blessed Jesus, bring your sacred Red Blood. Fill the Second Sphere with this eternal Cosmic Christ Protection.
3. Golden Buddha, bring your Flame of Wisdom. Fill the Third Sphere with Enlightenment and God-Victory.
4. Maha Chohan, bring the Green of Peace, abundance, plenty, and healing. Fill the Fourth Sphere with Manifestation of Power for perfect food, shelter, clothing, and the meeting of all human needs and appropriate desires.
5. Precious Mother Goddess, fill the Fifth Sphere with dazzling White Purity. Reflect back to me all less than the Holy Mother, for healing, with Absolute Love and Divine Compassion.
6. Ruby/Gold light of Lady Nada, fill the Sixth

Sphere with Devotion for God and absolute appreciation of life and my loved ones.

7. Saint Germain's Violet Flame, fill the Seventh Sphere with Joy. Transmute, pulsate, and dance, clearing absolutely all chaos from my aura, my environment, and my reality.

8. Rainbow Madonna, Lord Mary Buddha, bring the Raspberry Sherbet Fire of the Cosmic Mother to comfort, bless, and protect all Eight Spheres with the Light emanations of the Great Central Sun. They are thus sealed and enshrined by Alpha and Omega Omluminent Radiance.

9. Rainbow Sphere of Michael, condense to 7 feet. Rainbow Sphere of Michael, expand to 49 feet.* I Am now invincible, clear, and radiant. I Am a Solar Rainbow in Lord Michael's Loving Hands.

Archangel Lord Michael
Mary Clarice McChrist

---

* Play with your Rainbow Sphere. Learn when to close it and when to expand it out more fully.

Accept Your Divine Authority

Dear Children,

I Am your Brother and Protector, Lord Jesus, the Cosmic Christ. Calls for help are coming from humanity. Come together under My Divine Authority. There is no power but the Power of Light, the Power of Love.

I give unto each of you now the new Cosmic Power of My Divine Nature. You have the Authority which is transferred with these very words to command all less than the purest Christ Light to be transformed NOW by the Power of Love.

Take this dominion I offer to you NOW! Accept your Divine Authority! Take and embody the Seamless Garment of the Christ NOW. You are complete and protected NOW for all eternity.

Decree with me:

> "I take my dominion NOW in the Name of the Cosmic Christ, Jesus. I claim My Divine Authority over all less than the purest Christ Light. I cut all cords or connections with any anti-evolutionary energies. Archangel Michael, trace them all back to their source. Have them transformed by Divine Love NOW! By the Authority and Power of the Cosmic Christ, Jesus! It is so done."

Lord Jesus, the Cosmic Christ
Mary Clarice McChrist

Total Cosmic Christ Protection

I call on Cosmic Christ Jesus. (3x)

Through Cosmic Christ Jesus and through Mother Mary, I have God-Power over anything less than the purest Christ Light. (3x)

The Christ Light penetrates the darkness. (3x) All less than the purest Christ Light, transform and shift to the positive NOW. (3x)

The Christ Light permeates the darkness. (3x) All less than the purest Christ Light, transform and shift to the positive NOW. (3x)

The Christ Light saturates the darkness. (3x) All less than the purest Christ Light, transform and shift to the positive NOW. (3x)

In the Name and by the Authority of the Cosmic Christ Jesus, I command and demand that this healing be permanent, irrevocable, and stabilized by the Heart Flame of Mary and Jesus. So be it! (3x)

This prayer, which I say for myself, I say for all beings upon this Earth, and on all Earths in all time/space frames, past, present, and future. So be it!

I Am the White Seamless Garment of the Christ.

I Am healed! (3x)

So be it! It is so done!

Lord Jesus, the Cosmic Christ

Mary Clarice McChrist

The Inner Mysteries
Woodcut - 19th Century - by Unknown Artist

Book Two

The Inner Mysteries

Introduction to
The Inner Mysteries

Book Two of *The Blessed Mother's Blue Rose of the Healing Heart* is not for the uninitiated. It contains teachings given to me personally by beloved Christ Jesus, His Mother, and the Magdalene, over the past 30 years.

What is shared here is not found elsewhere. I have never seen these teachings in another book. I have shared these Mysteries only with one or two of my closest esoteric friends.

We are in the end times, and the world as we have known it is crumbling. This may be the last opportunity for me to unveil these teachings.

Book Two may present ideas and concepts which are new to you. You might react with shock, denial, or disbelief. It has taken me thirty years to accept and to integrate what Christ has personally taught me.

Denial is a powerful force within humans. It acts like a protective mechanism which allows you not to be overwhelmed or dismayed.

You do not need to accept these teachings if you are not ready to do so. Take what is written and symbolically place it on a shelf of your mind. Your logical thought process can only agree with those concepts which resonate with your own life experience.

When your heart has melted and your mind has

dealt with all its issues, you may wish to reopen, reread, and reflect once again upon these hidden mysteries. Perhaps it is best to say that these teachings are a parable, a story given to trigger your denial so that it can move. You are not asked to believe or to disbelieve these Truths.

Denial is the reaction to the parts of human experience which you could not process at the time. Perhaps it was too painful or too overwhelming to integrate, so your feelings were stuffed down, contracted into a tight ball of disbelief. This emotional energy which has not been processed is also referred to as *gapped energy*. It is part of your shadow self.

Today, Spirit is triggering you individually. Your hidden agendas are being exposed. Your old traumas, feelings, and experiences are starting to move again within your being and energy field. *These movements will allow the remnants of the Piscean Age to move off of you.* As you shift into higher and higher frequencies of Light, your willingness to be vulnerable will allow you to process all of your stuff and to let go of what no longer serves you.

If it is not loving expression, forgive yourself for not having dealt with it, and then, let it go!

In determining whether there is resonance for you related to a particular idea, concept, or teaching presented here, place it upon the altar within your heart. Let the Flames of Truth be your guide. Chills of Light, flowing through your body, will indicate an agreement from within your soul. Trust only what feels right to you.

Allow the rest to wait. It may not be time for you to understand or to work with a particular concept, idea, or teaching.

Your ability to assimilate higher levels of Truth is based on your level of Enlightenment. As your consciousness opens and expands, your ability to interpret life correctly will be vastly improved.

Let your heart and your Inner Knowing be your guide. It is extremely important to build your ability to discern what is right for you. It is also important not to judge things that you do not understand. Just set them aside; or, if they don't resonate with you, let them go. Set your intention to attract only that which is for your Highest Good.

I Am,

Mary Clarice McChrist

My Lady's Quest

In the pale moonlight
Across the sea
Comes the fair Princess
That looks for me.
In Her Eyes are the stories of all mankind.
Her Gift is Wisdom; I'll make Her mine.
When the white horse flies
With wings like snow
My Lady will rise and away She'll go.
To the Isle of Britain across the sea
My Lady comes to sup with me.
I'll know Her by Her Smile and Her Ring.
When my Lady comes, the birds will sing.
The knights will come to the Table Round.
From dreams, they know it will be found.
"Build the Fourth Round Table,
I now command.
"I Am Arthur, I claim this land."
Lord El Morya
Mary Clarice McChrist

I Serve The Grail
by Mary Sylvia McChrist

Chapter 1

The Holy Grail

The Holy Grail
A Legacy to Cherish

In approximately 560 AD, an experiment of Spirit manifested in the British Isles. Although historians argue the reality of King Arthur, it is important for you to see that this was an attempt to bring in a new Golden Age.

Camelot did not appear in a void. The lands of Britain had been previously imbued with the Flame of the Christ. Joseph of Arimathea, a tin merchant who regularly journeyed from Jerusalem to the British Isles, took his nephew, Jeshua ben Joseph (Jesus), to study with learned Druids there. Jesus took Initiations with these masters and etherically established the Flame which Arthur would rekindle in his lifetime. The purpose of Camelot was to bring forth a golden Christed Age of Chivalry, to uplift the feminine, and to establish Divine Order and justice in the lands of the British Isles.

The rich legacy of King Arthur, Guinevere, and the magical realm of Camelot carries ancient and symbolic patterns. The search for the Holy Grail became the court theme. This Mystical Cup was alleged to be the actual vessel which caught the precious blood of our Lord, Jesus Christ, at the Crucifixion.

Arthur's knights pursued the outer grail. Only Percival and Sir Galahad, son of Lancelot and Elaine, attained the Holy Grail. They actualized the Grail within themselves.

What was not known, is that both Percival and Sir Galahad carried the Lineage of the Holy Grail within their blood. Elaine was a descendant of the Christ through the Magdalene, as was her son, Sir Galahad, for the Sacred Blood Lines are carried by the mothers.

Although Camelot fell, the great experiment of creating Heaven on Earth had been taken a step further. Mistakes teach us much. Again and again, the Masters and Great Teachers try to guide humanity into a Golden Age.

The Lineage of the Holy Grail

The Soul Essence of both Mother Mary and Jesus has continued to reincarnate from the beginning of history upon this Earth. This genetic line is often referred to as the Lineage of the Holy Grail. This blood line of Christ was carried in royal ancestry as well as expressing in common lives. Both types of incarnations are important for learning the lessons necessary to master human life.

The Grail Lineage was passed through the mothers to their offspring. Those who carry this Lineage know who they are. They recognize others in this Christ family. Like the wildflowers of spring, the Grail family continues to reappear.

The Secret Order of the Blue Rose

The Order of the Blue Rose is a Secret Order which began in the Middle Ages. This was a time of unscrupulous male dominance over women. Even women in royalty were constantly challenged because they were female. The assumption was that they carried the Curse of Eve and could never think of being equal to a man.

Women were forbidden generally from owning property, having rights over their own bodies, their children, and their homes. If divorced, they were shamed and persecuted. They had no rights and no recourse to justice.

Most royal weddings were simply political maneuvers having nothing to do with love or free choice. Often, neither wife nor husband cared about the other.

Outside the castles, women's plight was even worse. Women were property and treated as such.

Mother Mary incarnated into a feminine body during this time period. She was asked by Spirit to begin the first Order of the Blue Rose. She was instructed to form this order in great secrecy. The women gathered under the guise of a sewing or knitting circle. When all servants were out of hearing range, the royal women got down to the true purpose of their gathering.

The tradition continued, as young women of royal blood were instructed by their mothers, aunts, and elder women who held a high spiritual focus. This became a place where Inner Realizations could be shared. The women discussed Blessed Mother Mary, Beloved Jesus, and His Love for Mary, the Magdalene. They learned that the Bible did not hold the entire Truth. The Blue Rose women wished to experience greater spiritual depth.

An old French manuscript, allegedly written by Mary Magdalene, revealed unknown information about the lives of Jesus, Mary, and the Magdalene. This and other Mysteries were passed down to generation after generation for about 500 years. The women in the Order of the Blue Rose took vows of death not to share the tenets of their order. The Blue Rose Order later went dormant and then magically would reappear as the Spring Rose.

This book, *The Blessed Mother's Blue Rose of the Healing Heart*, is in the tradition of the Blue Rose Order. Hold the teachings close to your heart.

Note on the Blue Rose:

Mother Mary continues to call forth many of Her Beloved Blue Rose Ladies by showing them the Blue Rose in their dreams and visions. If you have seen this, know Our Lady has personally called you to these Special Teachings. You are a member of this Sacred Order and will receive chills as you read this.

Chapter 2

White Madonna
Black Madonna

The White Madonna

Like Her Son, the Conception of Mary is veiled in mystery. Her mother, Anna, conceived the child Immaculately.

The Great Light came forth, penetrated Anna's womb etherically and she conceived a daughter. This child was destined to be the Mother of the Messiah.

Mary's Early Temple Training

Mary Anna was given to the Essene Temple of the Dove at the age of three. Anna, her mother, was the High Priestess of this temple. Mary and other young girls were prepared to receive the Messiah, for it was not known which young woman would be the mother of the Christ child.

The young maidens were instructed in purity, prayer, fasting, devotions, flower arranging, preparation of sacred oils, perfumes, healing, herbal remedies, and rituals. Sacred Sexuality was taught. Properly serving the husband was emphasized. Sexual Union was taught in the temple as a high level of spiritual devotion to God/Goddess. The women received instruction in respecting themselves as partners with God.

Please note that Mary and the twelve other young women in training to be the potential mother of the Messiah were all physical virgins. The girls not chosen to be the Beloved Mother would still be highly prized as brides in the Essene community when their temple years were completed.

In secret, Mary, the Maiden, was given special teachings by Helios, of the physical sun, and Archangel Gabriel in preparation for the Conception and Birth of the Messiah.

Only an initiate of the High Mysteries could hold the vibration necessary to bring forth the Son (Sun) of God.

Virgin Mary was taught to hold the Immaculate Concept for Her Son Emmanuel during Her Pregnancy. She held Him in thought as a pure and perfect Divine Image. It was this same Immaculate Concept that Mary later held/holds for all beings upon the Earth.

Mary the Lioness

Even when He was on the cross, Mary and the Magdalene continued to hold the Immaculate Concept of Christ's Perfection.

This fierce dedication of the Mother and the Magdalene helped Jesus endure the Crucifixion. It was after, when Jesus lay silent in the grave, that Mary broke down for three days and wailed to the Father God, "How dare You allow the killing of Your Son!" Mary stormed Heaven etherically and the Father Himself could not silence her.

"But wait, Mother, He will Rise. I have decreed it. The Christ will Rise!" assured the Father God. Mary later returned to Father God, Lord God

Adonai, who said, "Why are you here again, woman? You have beheld your Son. He is Risen. Why have you returned?"

"Yes, but it matters not. It takes not away from what He has suffered. Never, never again can this be allowed! You must promise me, Father. I shall not leave until I know that my Son is safe from future harm."

"Dear Mary, Mother of the Christ, lioness that you are, I shall solve this issue and put your heart at rest. *Never again shall the fullness of the Christ be gathered unto one body alone. For if that body should perish, the wholeness of humanity might be lost. I shall cause the duplication of the energy of My Son, Emmanuel.*

"He shall be placed in twelve bodies. Five who are Christ shall never be allowed to incarnate, and these shall remain eternally on the Inner Planes. Seven Christs shall I cause to descend. Five shall be male and two shall be female. These shall, for the most part, be hidden and unknown except unto a few. For you, dear Mother, could never be fooled. The mother lioness always knows her cubs."

"Will each of these Christs have the Powers of My Son?" asked Mary.

"Yes, but They shall be tested each time They incarnate into form. They must again receive the full Mantle of the Christ. Does this satisfy you, Mother?"

"Yes, I go in peace. Thank you, great Father God."

And so it was that Mary returned to Earth and

the stories of Christ Jesus' reappearance were heard in France, England, Tibet, Egypt, America, India, and beyond.

Even today many people feel they are an incarnation of Jesus the Christ. Remember that each person becomes "Christed" at the Transfiguration Initation. One could easily confuse this because the relationship to Christ is so profound. However, being an Embodiment of Christ Jesus is quite different (see pages 184-188).

The Black Madonna Lady of Mystery

O Lady of darkness, I honor thee.

O Lady of depth, enrich me.

Teach me patience and endurance.

Lift me over the jagged rocks.

Help me dissolve all the sorrow within me.

Help me transmute my shadow self.

Glorious Black Madonna,

Unveil to me your Sacred Mysteries.

Mary Clarice McChrist

Jesus and the Magdalene

The Magdalene was the Twin Flame of Christ. Mother Mary was His Twin Ray, meaning the highest level of the first separation of the soul and Spirit within the first etheric level of the 13th dimension of creation.

Much jealousy surrounded the life of Mary Magdalene. There is still much controversy about the Magdalene. Was she a saint or a sinner—priestess, goddess, healer, or prostitute? Whatever the historical fact, Jesus loved the Magdalene and has called her the Black Madonna. She held the Sacred Mysteries of the Void. She was symbolically one of the first women to confront her darkness, and she took Living Initiation with Jeshua (Jesus). She stepped through the veil of her own darkness and became the luminous expression of a Feminine Christ.

Mary, the Magdalene, and Jesus became confidants and formed a deep friendship of equals.

Following the Crucifixion of Jesus, the followers of Christ went underground. The Secret Mystery Teachings were only whispered.

The Black Madonna, Mother of the Void, is huge vast emptiness—the container of the unmanifest Mother—who is both darkness and sorrow. The Black Madonna has experienced it all: overcome life, death, rebirth. She continues on pouring out and emptying herself in an eternal stream of giving, birthing, and gathering again unto herself.

Even today, statues of the Black Madonna are hidden or gilded over by the Church because the image carries such a powerful focus of healing and regeneration. The people revere and adore the Dark Mother.

The Path of the Black Madonna is a difficult path, a lonely path, a path of sorrow, a way avoided by many. Yet, Mary Magdalene was Christ's Joy, His ecstasy, His Black Madonna.

Jesus Speaks to His Beloved

"O, My Mary, remember, in the beginning, before there was Light, there was darkness. You are that darkness. You are the Void, the unmanifest creation. I resides within your being.

"All that you are, I Am. In the Firmament of Heaven, there is no evil. Is the day good and the night, darkness, evil? No, Mary, it is all good.

"You are My Beloved, My Black Madonna. Let them talk and whisper against us. They are of this world. We are of the Heavens and beyond.

"As the priests of this world have misunderstood Me, so have the people condemned you and could not perceive your True Nature.

"I see you in all your glory and adore thee, as I adore God's whole Creation. Come with Me and let us be an example of the New Heaven and the New Earth. We outpictured the perfect Divine Union made not in this world, but a partnership created in Heaven and anchored upon this Earth. Let others see that we hold the Template for the Divine Relationship, one that shall remain the Holy Pattern for all time.

"You are the Void, the circle around Me. I Am the Light shining forth from the Firmament as the sun shines brightly from the sky. We cannot be separate, for we have been together since the beginning of time.

"Be My wife that we might fulfill this Great Love and establish our Love in this world."

"O My Lord, I Am only in Oneness with Thee. It shall be as You request. Wither Thou goest, I shall go, even if I never walk from this place. For You are established within me.

"You are Myself, the breath that enlivens this body. You are the motion that walks this form. You are the Love of All That Is; there is no one else but Thee, My Dear Lord."

And so it was, that Christ Jesus and Mary the Magdalene were married.

After the Crucifixion of Christ, the followers of Christ were not safe. Mary, Mother of Jesus, Mirium, Jesus' sister, Mary the Magdalene, and others sailed with Joseph of Arimathea to the land of France, where they met their Lord. The Inner Mysteries were carried in their hearts.

It is said that four children were born of the marriage of Jesus and Mary the Magdalene: two sons and two daughters. Two children were conceived physically and two were Conceived Immaculately.

The Grail Seed was thus planted through the Magdalene and the Christ in France in the Pyrenees Mountains, but the telling of this story awaits another time.

This Lineage was passed through succeeding generations through the mothers to the mother of King Arthur. King Arthur directly carried this Holy Grail Lineage.

The Miracle of the Thorn Tree

Miriam and the Holy Mother had traveled on to settle in the British Isles near the home of Joseph of Arimathea, Jesus' Uncle. Upon their arrival, Joseph planted his staff and a miracle occurred. The staff spontaneously blossomed and turned into a thorn tree.

Today, on Witherall Hill in Glastonbury, England, a similar thorn tree blossoms twice each year—once at Christmas and again during the advent of Easter.

Lord Jesus, the Cosmic Christ
Mary Clarice McChrist

Chapter 3

What is Embodiment?

Embodiment of Christ

> "Embodiment is the act of
> bringing the Higher Self into the physical form."
>
> Lord Maitreya

The Piscean Age was the Age of the Son and the Father. Jesus was always the Son of God, but He went through stages before He took on His full Mastery and His Mission as an Enlightened Healer and Shepherd for the children of Light.

When Jesus was Baptized, He became the Christ. Lord Maitreya overshadowed Him and worked through Christ Jesus' physical form. Later, Christ taught, "I and My Father are One!" He acknowledged Himself as One with the Father, God, The I Am That I Am.

This statement is very confusing for many people. Is there a difference between Christ and Jesus?

Yes. Jesus was a physical man who was an Avatar and World Teacher for the Piscean Age. The Christ is a level of Holy Perfection, a Mantle of Consciousness which all mankind is destined to embody. Humankind will be in Christ Consciousness by December 31, 2012. Jesus became the Christ after His Baptism. He is the Christ Matrix.

Many people called Jesus "God". Are Jesus and Father God the same? Christ Jesus was the great example. He laid out the Path of Discipleship and Divine Mastery for the Piscean Age and the 6th Root Race. He realized Himself as God; He became God-Realized. Because of this experience, He could say, "I and My Father are One," and "Before Abraham was, I Am."

He was not saying that there was not still the Source, but He had merged into the Creator and was at One with God forevermore. Thus, He was God-Realized.

Jesus embodied the Christ. Cosmic Lord Maitreya explains that Embodiment means to become or hold the energetic field of your higher aspect, the I Am Presence.

The higher you raise, the more aspects of yourself come into Oneness with you. Symbolically, you become larger and larger until you are One with everything.

The title "Lord Jesus, the Cosmic Christ" indicates a Being far beyond Jeshua Ben Joseph, the beautiful young master Jesus who was Baptized by John the Baptist.

The Shepherd has laid out the Pathway for all beings. Therefore, Embodiment is our destiny.

Mary Clarice McChrist

The Embodiment of the Divine Mother

Mary Clarice McChrist

The keynote of the Piscean Age was, "I and my Father are One." Today, in this Age of the Mother, the appropriate mantra is :"I and my Mother are One!"

My work is to bring forth the Immaculate Concept of the Divine Mother God. I organized the First Conclave of the Mother in 1993. Few people had even heard of the Divine Mother or Goddess in America. Now, most awakened women know themselves as representatives of the Divine Feminine. Events for the Mother or the Goddess are now common.

Embodiments—incarnations of Mother—are readily accepted if the women are of East Indian heritage. *It is time to recognize that the Divine Mother incarnates into all races and nationalities.*

Being a Divine Mother is a job description. It is the person's Mission. *Mother Mary said that there are twenty-two embodiments of Herself on the Earth now. Two of these incarnations are men.*

"I multiply myself through these Divine Mother Beings. They are My Heart, My Hands, and My Feet. They are incarnate to Serve the children of Light and to complete My Work."

Recent teachings by Lord Maitreya point out that

the destiny of each Central Soul and Spirit (Parental Soul) (Glosssary, page 233) is to embody your own I Am Self. This means that more Divine Mothers, Father Gods, and Ascended Masters will be appearing on Earth!

The Essence of the Higher Being at first moves in and out of your form, as you, the physical vehicle, are prepared to hold higher frequencies and energy fields. The mental body and consciousness are greatly expanded. Your Temple is being prepared.

Emotionally, the adjustment is often most difficult. Are you worthy? Accepting your own Divinity and your specific missions or dharma can be very challenging. What a privilege it is to experience the self as your Higher Self or even the Mother, the Father, the Christ, or the Buddha.

What Will You Embody?

The Mother or Goddess is destined to anchor within all beings, both masculine and feminine. If your life work is also with Mother Mary, Goddess Quan Yin, the Black Madonna, or Bridget, for examples, then there is a slight possibility you are becoming the Divine Mother. This is different then just anchoring the Mother, because it means that your Higher Self is actually a Divine Mother. *You can only become who your already Are.* An acorn grows into an oak tree rather than a rose. If your Higher Self is a Divine Mother, then you will eventually become Her.

As the Divine Mother you will service the children because that is your Life Mission.

If your work focuses on Saint Germain or another Ascended Master, you are probably in the process of becoming that Being, or more likely, you are in their Soul Band, which means They are responsible for you and your progress. The Master must ascend all members of His or Her Soul Band or Family.

There are millions of beings and missions. They are all important to the collective goal of Ascending the Earth.

All beings who are a body of the Mother or an Ascended Master are also real people who go through pain, trials, and grief, just as everyone else does. When your Higher Self embodies in your form— no longer withdraws, but has anchored the Electronic Presence within your form—you are rightly called an Embodiment.

Embodiment is a sacred and natural process of realizing who you already Are. In the Golden Age, this process will be supported and encouraged by members of your spiritual community. *Each Embodiment will be a celebration of a new God-Being in form.*

Today, sadly enough, this is not the case. A dear friend recently announced that he is one of the well known Ascended Masters. Although his announcement has been celebrated in one of the European countries, here in his home town, he was judged and even driven out of his apartment by one irate non-believer. Some outside people may consider that he is just in his ego, or that he is crazy to feel that he could really be an Ascended Master. You usually have to be experiencing your own Embodiment to realize that it is actually possible to become the Higher Self.

What I observed was that my friend is definitely a "body of the Master." When the Master spoke through him, his voice changed and his aura increased dramatically, yet he wasn't really channeling. I think he is in the process of embodying, but the Master may not yet be stabilized in his form. Timing is critical.

If you have accomplished the sacred task of Embodiment, I ask for your God-Self and Council of Light to send you chills or your truth signal as you read this passage.

If Embodiment has not yet been accomplished, I recommend the *Practice of the Flaming Hearts of Mary and Jesus*. This will bless you and speed up your Initiation Process.

Embodiment is a sensitive issue. As part of your Initiation Process, it is important to "announce yourself", but, in today's world, this may still be dangerous, so be careful.

I Am *Mary Clarice McChrist*

Mary of the Flaming Heart
Woodcut - 19th Century - Artist Unknown

Chapter 4

The Flaming Hearts

Flaming Hearts of Mary and Jesus

Flaming Hearts of Mary and Jesus,
You are eternally One with me.
Divine Mother and Son of Great Perfection,
Unify within my soul today.

Burn from my heart all pain.
Let sorrow move freely through me.
Let my tears flow and allow me to heal
All illusions in my life.

Sadness and joy, ignorance and wisdom,
Death and life, burn all polarity.
Fires of freedom, sing within my heart.
I surrender to Thy Flame of Bliss.

O my Precious Christ, O my Sweet Mother,
Flaming Hearts of Mary and Jesus,
I invoke You with Joy,
For I experience your perfect Union.

I Am Lord Mary

Mary Clarice McChrist

Becoming the Flaming Heart Practice

Introduction

"The Practice for becoming the Flaming Heart is My most profound teaching."

Lord Mary

What is the Flaming Heart? The Flaming Heart is seen in many paintings of Mary and Jesus. This Sacred Heart is the loving consciousness of Holy Fire. It is symbolic of the Living Flame of the Source Mother-Father which burns eternal in the Tabernacle of the Lord of Hosts.

Few Saints and Sages have achieved this Flaming Heart. It is a Gift of Grace given as one reaches a high level of purity and devotion. You can prepare your body to receive this Gift, but you cannot achieve the Flaming Heart until you have embodied your Divine Purpose, Mission, and Higher Self, for the Power of the Heart is the greatest Power in the Cosmos.

If you have accomplished this sacred task, I ask that your Council of Light send to you chills, or your own truth signal, as you read this passage.

This is my Gift to humanity through Mary Clarice McChrist.

I Am Divine Mother Mary, Queen of Peace

Mary Clarice McChrist

Preparing the Heart

Beloved Children,

I Am Mary, Mother of all People. Today, I come to share My Heart with you. Come, My children, into My Great Flaming Heart. We are Eternal in Oneness.

"Closer than hands and feet Am I." Beloved Christ has told us.

> "I Am your breath flowing
> through your body."
>
> "I Am the Oneness of the heart."
>
> "I Am the Flaming Heart of
> Mary and Jesus."
>
> "I Am in Oneness with you."

The Golden Heart Door

Go into your heart. Drop your consciousness from your head down into the center of your being, your heart center. Focus there; be there now!

Feel your heart. Imagine (pretend) a tiny golden door which you now open. You enter easily, just as Alice entered Wonderland.

What do you experience? Feel it. Look carefully around. Are you indoors? Is there an altar? Are there sacred objects or artifacts?

Be totally present and experience your surroundings.

Find the Crucible of your Heart. See the Three-Fold Flame there: Blue for the Will of the Father, Gold for the Wisdom of the Son/Daughter, and Pink for the Love of the Mother.

What size are the Flames? If you cannot see them, feel them or pretend that they exist within you.

Is one color larger than the rest?

What does that mean?

Take a fan—one you instantly manifest—and fan the flames. Blow on them. Allow them to grow. Use your intention to alter their size. Prepare them to receive the Flaming Heart of Mary and Jesus.

Now, beloved, go into Stillness; meditate before the Flames. Breathe slowly, feel your I Am Presence merged within you. Meditate here as long as possible. Feel your Peace and Joy expand.

As previously mentioned, this will not happen until you have reached a high degree of Grace. If you are serious about attaining the Flaming Heart, work with this meditation daily.

Remember, you cannot achieve the Flaming Heart until you have embodied your Divine Purpose, Mission, and Higher Self.

Mother Mary, Queen of Peace
Mary Clarice McChrist

I Am The Flaming Heart of Mary and Jesus

Ceremony of Healing and Initiation

For maximum benefit from this experience, step out of your mind, focus in your heart, and surrender to your I Am Presence.

Candles are lit for each color of the Flames called forth in the ceremony. The leader will read brief sections; group responses will be indicated.

Leader: Call forth Spirit.

"I call forth the Sisterhood and Brotherhood of the Ray of the Ascended Christ, Beloved Divine Mother Mary, Beloved Lord Jesus, all Archangels, all Elohim, all Councils of Light in the Great White Lodge, the three teams of Emissaries of Light--the Pleiadian Emissaries of Light, the Sirian Archangelic League of Light, the Andromedan Emissaries of Light, Raphael, the Healers of the Emerald Cross, and the Healers of the Rosie Cross."

Please repeat with me:

"In the Name of Jesus, the Christ, I call all less than the Purest Christ Energy to be transmuted with Purest Love and shifted from the 4th to the 5th dimension Now."

Leader:

"The Flames of Jesus are Blue, Purple, and Gold. Blue represents the Father's Will. Purple carries the royal estate of the I Am Presence. Gold is infinite abundance and Grace."

Please repeat with me:

"Flames of Jesus, rise and whirl.
Flames of Jesus, now unfurl." (3x)

Leader:

"The Flames of Mary are Pink, Raspberry, and Silver. Pink shifts all to Love. Raspberry creates joy, wisdom, and depth of intuition. Silver transmutes instantly and removes all dross."

Please repeat with me:

"Flames of Mary, rise and blaze.
Flames of Mary, Mother raise." (3x)

Leader: Working the Flames:

"Flames of Jesus, cleanse and heal.
Flames of Jesus, all Light reveal.
Dance and blaze within my core,
Cleanse my bodies forevermore."

Please repeat with me:

"Flames now lift and blaze me through.
O Flames, bring Peace in all I do."(3x)

Blue Flame

Leader:

"See Blue Flames beginning at your head and slowly working through your entire body. I call the Brothers and Sisters of the Ray of the Ascended Christ to place cones above and below: you, your home, and this temple, to carry away all unwanted energy. Any dense energy is removed by Spirit as we speak."

Please repeat with me:

"Within my heart I see Blue. I feel the Will of God wishing to heal me completely.

"The Will is actually the feminine quality of God, though in the Piscean Age we were taught it was masculine.

"My intention is to completely align my self with the Will of God in this moment and for all time. I Am worthy and God desires me to heal spontaneously. All less than God's perfection now cease to exist!

"I reflect the Perfect Will of God. Every cell and atom of myself is perfect, whole, and at Peace now in the Name of the Mother-Father."

Leader:

"The Blue stays within the physical form."

Gold Flame

Leader:

"Imagine Gold Flames in your heart chakra. See Golden Flames concentrating in the heart and then moving outward, now penetrating all your auric bodies. The Gold goes out six feet from the body, cleansing the body and the auric field."

Repeat with me:

"I Am the Golden Light of the Christ and the Buddha. I Am, now and forever, Gold working and transforming my life into abundance and ease. I manifest all I require with ease and Grace.

"So be it!"

Purple Flame

Leader:

"Purple is the royal color of kings and queens. It denotes royalty and stands for the Divinity of the I Am Presence. Imagine your mid-heart is filled with Purple Flames now. These Flames emanate from a great Purple Gem which carries the royalty of the Davidic Line. This Line flows through the Family of the Holy Grail and through the Beloved I Am Self, moving freely into the physical body-temple."

Repeat with me:

"Beloved I Am Presence, I adore thee!" (3x)

Leader:

"Feel the Purple Flames blaze up, in, and through yourself. Feel the subtlety of the Purple Flames."

Please repeat with me:

"I Am of the Lineage of David.

I carry the Lines of Christ.

I Am Christ in form.

I instantly transmute all my life

With the Essence of the Inner Christ.

I Am That I Am."

Mary's Flames: Pink Flame

Leader:

"See Pink Light in your mid-heart area. Ask Mother Mary to open your heart with ease and Grace."

Please repeat with me:

"All less than Mary's Love is transmuted instantly in this moment. (3x)

"Divine Mother Mary, assist me now."

Leader:

"Mary, bring delicate Pink Feathers to whisk free our hearts.

"Feel the Feathers sweep through your heart, cleansing and healing all less than Mother's Love."

Please repeat with me:

"I Am a great Pink Flame. Flames, move through me completely from my feet to my crown. Angels of the Pink Flame, bring your Healing Ministry."

Leader:

"Work with this Light for three to seven minutes as required.

"Thank you, Mary, and the Pink Angelic Hosts."

Raspberry Flame

Leader:

"O Raspberry Flames of Joy, Light of the Cosmic Mother, blaze through me now! Expand my chest to receive your Joy.

"Stretch your chest. Arch your back. Open up the front of the chest. Bend over. Allow your arms to extend forward, stretching. Then stretch arms behind back, and stretch forward. Lift up the neck with eyes upward and stretch out your back. Allow the Raspberry Light to work with the body."

Silver Flame

Leader:

"Silver Flames of Mother Mary, shift instantly all energy brought up in my auric field.

"Sit, stand, or get on all fours. The Silver Light will begin at your head and work down through your form. Work arms in backward circles, loosening and transmuting dense energy. Run it down your spine and then through your head, then slowly throughout each chakra and through your entire form. Feel the body grow lighter and lighter."

Again, Raspberry Flame

Leader:

"Bring the Raspberry Flame back again to bring in the Joy."

Please repeat with me:

"Raspberry Flame, blaze and blaze:

Bring the Joy for me to raise." (3x)

Leader:

"A dimensional shift is happening now. Feel it. Your body may shake or release in some way. You may yawn which means your vibration is increasing. This is fine, and means the process is working for you."

Meditation with the Flames

Leader:

"Please close your eyes: Mother Mary now draws up Her Flames of Pink, Raspberry, and Silver into your heart. Jesus now draws up His Flames of Blue, Purple, and Gold into your heart.

"We will now meditate with these Flames and allow each of you to have your own meditative experience for 5 to 10 minutes. *Use your breath to fan the flames in your heart.* This is a powerful mystical practice, worthy of your individual attention. See the Flames expand and grow in intensity. Become the Flaming Hearts of Mary and Jesus."

Green Flame

Leader:

"Now, to end this ceremony, I call in the Green of Mother Earth and thank Her for Her support of all life. This Green now floods our bodies and auric fields.

"Blessed Mother Earth, thank you for allowing life to be within your nature. Thank you for your brooks of grace and beauty, your noble mountains like Mt. Shasta, your green fertile valleys, and your wild jungles and rain forests. I support you, and you support me. I will pray for your renewal and support by bringing beauty to my part of the world."

Group repeats:

"O Green Light, bring integration and healing to this process. Thank you, Beloved Gaia."

Leader:

"We feel the Green of Mother Earth flowing up our feet, legs, buttocks, chakras: 1st - base, 2nd - sexual chakra, 3rd - solar plexus, 4th - heart, 5th - throat, 6th - 3rd eye, and 7th - crown chakra. The

Green bathes, heals, and integrates all of our energies.

"Work with this Green Light for about three minutes".

Repeat with me:

"With my strong intention, I now fully accept this clearing and healing with full God-Power. I rejoice, for I Am now holding the Flames of Lord Mary and Lord Jesus in my heart, right now, and forevermore. (3x)

"So Be It! So Mote It Be!"

Leader:

"By the Power vested in me by beloved Cosmic Christ Jesus and Lord Mary, I call this ceremony finished. We thank all of the Beloved Ones of Spirit who have assisted us this day/evening. We disconnect now and give appreciation for your co-creation with those of us in form. Thank you, beloved Lord Jesus and Mother Lord Mary."

Group repeats:

"We love you. (3x)

"We bless you. (3x)

"So Be It!

"Shanti Shanti Shanti."

Leader:

"Would anyone like to share your experience?

(People share.)

"Please come join together in a circle to offer praise. We will go around the circle, allowing each one who wishes, to add a word or sentence of Praise.

"You may wish to begin with, 'My word of Praise is...'

(People give their words of Praise.)

"Afterwards, we will seal this ceremony with three OMs.

(OMs given in unison.)

"Thank you for coming and participating with us this evening. Please give everyone a big hug."

I Am Mary, Your Mother

Mary Clarice McChrist

The Accolade
by E.B. Leighton - 19th Century England

Chapter 5

The Secret Mysteries

The Six Secret Mysteries

The Mystery of Giving
The Mystery of Forgiving
The Mystery of Multiplying
The Mystery of the Black Madonna
The Mystery of the White Madonna
The Mystery of the One

The Secret Mysteries

The Six Secret Mysteries

I, Lord Mary, promised the giving of Six Secret Mysteries to my daughter Mary McChrist, when she had reached the Purity to receive these Initiations. This night, March 3, 2001, at this time, in the depth of the Tribulation, I open My Essence and pour out My Pearls of Great Price.

These Mysteries are not meant for the young lambs, for they will not understand and will continue to search for the Outer Shepherd. These Mysteries are not meant for the wolves, who seek only to take and confound the pure of heart.

This Gift is for you, the wise ones, who followed the Shepherd until His Path penetrated your heart, until you absorbed the Christ, became the Christ, ate His Last Supper, drank His Wine, knew His Inspiration, and broke His Bread, His body, sharing it amongst all people.

Are you this one? Are you My Son, My Daughter, in whom I Am well pleased? Then come with Me now and receive My New Covenant before the time for this Sacred Teaching is passed. For this Earth shall be passed away. In the twinkling of an eye, I come forth with My Son, Jesus. In the twinkling of an eye, we shall be gone, and the

Earth, as She is now, shall be gone with Us.

This is not a dissolution or an ending. This is the Ascension from this plane of existence—a clearing, dissolving, a melting of the old, and an uplifting, expanding, loving in the New. Be not afraid. Even now, I Am with you, dear ones. Everything you will ever accomplish is done. Every hope, fear, every caress, every kiss is completed. There are no words to say nor things to do. Only rest with Me in Oneness.

This is the natural state. Simplicity covers us all as a Garment of Peace.

Let go. I Am you.

I Am Lord Mary

The First Mystery
The Mystery of Giving

Giving is the Role of the Master, the Mother, the Father of All That Is. Giving is receiving. You who give not, know not Love. You who give shall receive all that is laid before you.

The Second Mystery
The Mystery of Forgiving

The Christ forgave those who persecuted and killed Him. This settled all karma between Him and His adversaries. This allowed Christ's Soul and Body to Ascend.

All that is in, of, or that which appears confined to this Earth is now freed up, through forgiveness, to move, to balance, to heal. With forgiveness of yourself and others, all is possible. Your karma is done—complete— now and forever, world without end.

I Am That I Am!

The Third Mystery
The Mystery of Multiplying

The multiplying of the loaves and fishes by Christ Jesus established the Matrix of Abundance for all beings and for all times.

As you are created in the image and likeness of Christ, of God/Goddess/All That Is, you have every right to inherit the Kingdom. This means all is given unto you in thoughts, ideas, inspiration, and the material manifestation of what you hold in your consciousness.

Mother-Father God gives all unto you. Know that this is so. Give thanks, bless Us as We bless you. Bless all your family and the family of man. As the 5th dimension is revealed, you will create instantly. Master your images, your desires, and your deepest shadow self. Be purified, born again. Be as My Child: pure, wholesome, a Child of Faith. And yet be an adult: a daughter/son of God/Goddess.

What does this mean, My children? Take what you have, and bless it daily!

"I bless you in the Name and by the Power of the Christ Jesus, the King." Christ and God are One, indivisible. God blessed humanity and told you to multiply.

A circle represents a full blessing of giving and receiving. You manifest in a circle. It is that simple.

Give Joy and reap Joy.

Give service and reap service.

Give money and reap money.

The circle, O, is the Power of the One!

The Fourth Mystery
The Mystery of the Black Madonna

Woman is womb-man. She is Goddess, Creator of all. She is the Void, the unmanifest potential of All That Is.

Man intuitively knows this, and it frightens him. He feels inadequate to manage woman, for she holds the Mystery of Creation within her and she knows it. Woman has been held down because she is Power!

Mother God is the Circle.

Father God is the Dot.

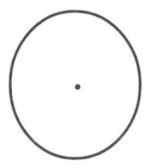

The Circle is the Womb of the Great Mother. This is a great Mystery. Contemplate this sincerely. God the Father is the Dot of Stillness within.

Mary Magdalene is the Black Madonna. By facing your shadow and dealing with it completely, you overcome yourself and reveal the creative potential of your own God Power.

When you are unafraid of the darkness, you will face it and can erase all duality. It is in the Center, like the Dot within Mother God, that you are protected, and, at the same time, all-powerful—for there are no opposites within you.

Like Mary Magdalene, you may be accused or even condemned. The Christ said to His Beloved, "Remember, Mary, before there was Light there was Darkness."

"Where is he who has accused you, woman?"

Christ keeps and unfolds all Inner Mysteries.

The Fifth Mystery
The Mystery of the White Madonna

The virgin body is not possible without virgin consciousness. The White Madonna is the part of you that holds your Immaculate Divine Blueprint. No matter what is outpictured in your reality, the Truth holds firm. That Truth is who you are.

The Tribulation comes forth. It has its experiences—its *lila* or Divine Play—yet all is already accomplished.

The White Madonna is Our Lady. She embodies all Light, all Love, all Goodness. She is also within you.

I and My Mother are One.

Accept your Purity.

The Final Mystery
The Mystery of the One

Beloved Ones,

Everything is in Oneness. Appearances are illusions. Separation is unreal and therefore nonexistent.

Individual consciousness transits from black to white, from darkness to Light. When duality is seen as merely illusion, then Oneness is experienced. Your consciousness moves, soaring up and out, as the vibration expands. There is only Infinite Oneness.

The Self experiences itself as God, the One.

I Am Alpha and Omega,

The beginning and the end.

The full circle brings us back to Center—

Which is All That Is.

The Truth is ONE!

I Am that Truth!

I Am that Truth!

So be it!

Homage to the White Madonna

The Virgin Mary is the White Madonna. Like Tara in Buddhism, Durga in Hinduism, Isis in Egyptian religion, and White Buffalo Calf Woman in Native American tradition, the White Madonna holds the place of the Divine Mother.

Virgin Mary is utter Purity, almost unattainable. She is beyond what we expect for ourselves, and yet we must strive to be Mary, Mother of God. *For She is a powerful model for women and men alike.* The White Madonna embodies our Highest Ideal: a human mother who is the Mother of God, the Cosmic Mother in all Her Glory.

> We pray to Her; She offers us Grace.
> We cry out; She soothes our tears.
> We despair; She comforts us.
> She holds us in Her Heart and we heal.

> O Mary, accept us as Your children.
> Uplift us into Your Holy Estate
> That we might become You, Blessed Mother,
> You who hold the Christ within.
> You who encompass all beings,
> All worlds, in Your Holy Essence.

> O Mary, we Love You, as You Love us,
> Without separation or boundary.
> This Love is as Eternal as are we.

> Mary, O Mary, O Mary.

Appendix
of Sacred Music

"I have found these selections very inspiring in the creation of the ambiance for the Blue Rose gatherings."

Mary Clarice McChrist

Music to Set the Energetic Field for a Spiritual Gathering

Erik Berglund, Eight albums. See: *Angel Chants* and *Somewhere* with *Ave Maria*. Erik Berglund, P. M. B. 35, Mt. Shasta Blvd., Mt. Shasta, CA 96067. Order from web site: www.erikberglund.com

Dwain Briggs, *Echoes of a Modern God* © 1998, Merkaba Music. Especially recommended are *One God* and *Peace Prayer*. 7985 Santa Monica Blvd., Ste. 189-271, West Hollywood, CA 90024

Michael Maxwell, *Elegance of Pachelbel, Cannon in D Minor*. Please order from the web site: www.avalonmusic.com

Kurt Van Sickle, *Mother Divine* © 1994, 1SUN Music, P.O. Box 141217, Austin, TX 78714

Kurt Van Sickle, *Make Me an Instrument* © 1994, 1SUN Music, P.O. Box 141217, Austin, TX 78714

Richard Souther, *Angel Vision, The Music of Hildegard Von Bingen*, S21-8449

Music to Our Lady

Paul Armitage, *Our Lady of All Nations Peace Garden* © 2000. CD available through the Mother Matrix P. O. Box 1178, Mt. Shasta, CA 96067. The music was created as a soul portrait for the Our Lady of All Nations Peace Garden, $16.95, (530) 235-4117

Judy Armstrong, *Let Your Heart Sing* © 1994, T & J Productions, P.O. Box 973, Nanton, Alberta, Canada T0L 1R0, Phone: (403) 646-5519

Joel Andrews, *Ave Maria, Ave Maria Meditation*, CD or cassette, order through web site: www.jps.net/goldharp/new.html

Celine Dion, *These Are Special Times* © 1998, *Ave Maria - The Prayer*

Mario Lanza, *Ave Maria* from *The Most Classical Christmas Album Ever*, BMG/RCA Victor #63712 9/26/2000

Barbara Streisand, *A Christmas Album, Ave Maria* and *Our Father - The Lord's Prayer,* Columbia 9557 (CO), Oct, 1967

Richard Shulman & Connie Stardancer, *Awake, Arise, Ascend* © 1992, especially *The Great Invocation* and *Hail Mary (Blessed Ascension Rosary,* Mary McChrist, set to music) Richeart Music, P. O. B. 457, Woodstock, NY, 12498, (888) 699-3682, www.richeartmusic.com

Richard Shulman, *Keeper of the Holy Grail, Light Music to Clear, Align the Chakras, Music to Walk the Labyrinth* and *Camolot Reawakened: A Vision Fulfilled,* Richeart Music, P. O. B. 457, Woodstock, NY, 12498, (888) 699-3682, web site: www.richeartmusic.com

The Mother/Goddess

Cecelia, *Voice of the Feminine Spirit*, especially *Amazing Grace*, Phonographic Performance Ltd., Ganton House, 14-22 Ganton St., London, WTV 1LB, UK

Robert Gass, *Ancient Mother, Kyrie,* and *On Wings of Song,* Spring Hill Press, 5216 Sunshine, Boulder, CO 80302

Galalisa Star, *Om Ma Shawta* (chant), *Euphoria*, and *Sri Ma,* 2533 105th St. SW, Apt 101, Edmonton, AB, T6J4T5, Canada, call (780) 487-4522, or please e-mail: galalisa@aol.com

Lisa Thiel, *Lady of the Lake, Journey to the Goddess, Invocation to the Graces* and *Mother of Compassion,* Sacred Dream Productions, 223 Jasmine Ave. Monrovia, CA, 81916, e-mail: info@ladyslipper.org, (800) 634-6044. Order from web site : www.ladyslipper.org

Kathy Zavada, *Mother's 'Song, In Love Divine, Journey Home* and *I'm Right Here,* from Precious Music, Contact: P.O. Box 531, Mt. Shasta, CA 96067, web site: www.kathyzavada.com

Lovely Music

Patrick Bernhardt, *Atlantis Angelis* from Production Atlantis Angelis, Division de Groupe Quebecor, Inc., 7033 Route Trans Canadienne, St. Laurent (Quebec) H4T 1S2, Canada

Buddy Comfort, *Brother Sun, Sister Moon,* Tellurion Records, P.O. Box 1123, Sebastopol, CA 95473, toll free telephone: (888) 459-5827, web site: www.soft-light.com/buddy/order.htm

Aryeh David, *Love's Whisper* © 1998 (AR1100), P. O. Box 219, Talent, OR 97540

Handel's Messiah,Vol. 5 Christmas Classics, © 1992, Metacon Inc., *Hallelujah* (calls in Lord Jesus the Christ)

Mt. Shasta Anthology © 1999, world-class local artists, Musical Pathways, P.O. Box 1222, Mt. Shasta, CA 96067, web site: www.musicalpathways.com

Deva Premal, *Love Is Space*, from White Swan Music, 1705 14th St. #143, Boulder, CO 80302, (303) 527-8770, e-mail: swan@nettone.com

James Twyman, *Emissary of Light, Songs from the Peace Concerts* © 1997, Band Together Records, 2226 East Lake Ave. E 119, Seattle, WA 98102. Order from web site: www.BandTogether.com

A Powerful Experience

Michael Stillwater, *Graceful Passages, A Companion for Living and Dying* © 2000, Companion Arts, P.O. Box 2528, Novato, CA 94949-2528. Please see web site: www.wisdomoftheworld.com, (888) 242-6608

Mother Mary Teachings

Ileah, *Mother Mary's Teachings for the New World* © 2002, Fourteen of Mary McChrist's prayers are included on this CD. Please see our web site: www.bluedolphinpublications.com, e-mail: bdolphin@netshel.net

Glossary of Divine Beings

Adonai Tsebayoth - Holy Father, Lord God of Hosts, Father of Lights. The words "Adonai Tsebayoth" cause the dissolving of all negative energy and may be used as a mantra, a repeated prayer.

Archangels - created by God, the Light of Infinite Being. There are 7 Archangel pairs and 5 Secret Ray Archangel partners:

    Blue, Ray 1, **Michael and Faith**

    Yellow, Ray 2, **Jophiel and Christine**

    Pink, Ray 3, **Chamuel and Charity**

    White, Ray 4, **Gabriel and Hope**

    Green, Ray 5, **Raphael and Lady Regina***

    Ruby/Bold, Ray 6, **Uriel and Donna Grace**

    Violet, Ray 7, **Zadkiel and Holy Amethyst**

Archangel Michael (Mikael) - "Who is as God," Lord of Protection and Champion of the Innocent. Call Archangel Michael to bring forth His Flaming Blue Sword and clear your body and environment of any vibration less than the purest Christ Light.

Black Madonna - The transmuter of world suffering, Lady of the Void, the unmanifested Creation before there was Light. Lord Jesus also called Mary Magdalene His Black Madonna, His Beloved One.

---

*Mother Mary now serves as the Divine Mother and Cosmic Mother, so Lady Regina is assisting Archangel Raphael.

Buddha - Prince Siddhartha Gautama became the Buddha. He and Lord Jesus are spiritual brothers. God sent Lord Gautama (the Buddha) to the people of the East to show that their Enlightenment could be achieved through mental and moral purification, the Middle Way. Jesus and Buddha continue to work together for the benefit of all beings on Earth.

Cosmic Mother - An office of the Spiritual Hierarchy. Lord Mary, Queen of Peace, Quan Yin, Goddess of Mercy, and Lord Mary Buddha are the Triad of the Cosmic Mother. They oversee all life on Earth and throughout the cosmos.

Dove of Peace - The feminine Holy Spirit, also called Holy Soul, which anoints humanity and uplifts consciousness into Oneness with the Christ/Father. The Divine Breath, the Third Person, which should be called upon to bless a human love relationship or marriage. The Mother Christos is also the Dove of Peace.

Elohim - The builders of form. They are referred to in the *Bible*. They implemented part of God's Creation by creating mountains, continents and oceans. They are the evolutionary top of the Elemental Kingdom.

There are 6 original sets of Elohim Twins:

Blue, Ray 1	Hercules
	Amazonia
Yellow, Ray 2	Apollo (Service began in 1959.)
	Lumina
Pink, Ray 3	Heros (Orion)
	Amora (Angelica)

White, Ray 4	Purity
	Astrea (Claire)
Green, Ray 5	Cyclopea (Vista)
	Virginia (Crystal)
Ruby/Gold, Ray 6	Peace
	Aloha
Violet, Ray 7	Arcturus
	Victoria

God, Mother-Father God - God expresses in Oneness, in polarity and as a Trinity. God is both Mother— Divine Will, Love, and Wisdom—and Father—Divine Power, Authority, and Protection. God is Truth, Love, Life, the One Mind, the Holy Spirit.

Guides - Etheric beings who guide your personal progress. These beings are always with you either consciously or unconsciously. Your Primary Guide is responsible for your spiritual progress and the completion of your Mission.

The Holy Spirit - Traditionally, the third member of the Divine Trinity is without gender, or is both feminine and masculine, depending on circumstances. For clarity sake, we are defining Holy Spirit as masculine, and the Holy Soul as feminine. Holy Soul is also the Dove of Peace.

I AM Presence - The Higher Self, your individualized God Self, which includes levels of the Christ, Buddha, Mother and the Father. Each level descends into your form as you pass higher and higher levels of Initiation. *We must descend, before we ascend.*

I AM THAT I AM - The name of each person's God-nature or Mother-Father God Self. "The God of your fathers hath sent me unto you. What is His name?" "And God said unto Moses, I AM THAT I AM." (Exodus 3:13, 14)

Lord Jesus, The Cosmic Christ - This title was given Our Lord on December 31, 1991, as His sphere of influence reached an even higher level within the Cosmos. *Jesus Christ was the Highest Divine Expression in human form during the Piscean Age.* He is the Cosmic Christ of All That Is. He prepared a Pathway for humanity to follow.

His life was an example of the spiritual stages of initiation: Birth, Baptism, Transfiguration, the Garden, Crucifixion, Resurrection, and Ascension. By living and transcending these tests and stages, humanity truly follows Our Lord and becomes the Risen Christ. (Refer to *The Keys To The Golden Age* by Mary Clarice McChrist.)

Lord Mary - The name given by the Spiritual Hierarchy to Mother Mary on December 31, 1991, to denote Her shift in authority from an earthly to a cosmic level. She holds a position in the Trinity of the Cosmic Mother.

Lord Mary Buddha - The Rainbow Madonna, a representation of Mary on the sixth Buddhic Level of Being. She is the Dove of Peace, the Phoenix risen from the fires of experience to become the perfect Immaculate Concept of Being. Lord Mary Buddha holds your Perfection within Her Heart. She holds a position in the Trinity of the Cosmic Mother.

Lord Metatron (El Sheddai) Grand Chancelor of Heaven, Prince of the Divine Face or Presence. He who resides closest to the Throne of God. He may be called upon for protection, abundance, and deliverance from death. He is said to be the angel who led the Children of Israel after the exodus. Lord Metatron, Lord Michael, and Lord Melchizedek work as a Triune Principle under the Supreme God.

Lord Michael - Lord Michael was born directly from the Supreme Mother's Heart. Jesus Christ is of Michael's Spiritual Lineage. Lord Michael's Essence was incarnated as Christ Jesus, as the Avatar of the Piscean Age.

Lord Michael is also known as Christ Michael. Archangel Michael is a Great Aspect of Lord Michael. He embodies Divine Will and Power in this universe and holds the position of Protector for the Children of Light. Call upon Michael for clearing and protection.

Lord St. Germain - Lived as Joseph, the protector of the Christ Child. He was Merlin, Columbus, and a familiar figure in the European courts for over 600 years. He was the leading Master Presence inspiring the Founding Fathers of the United States of America in 1776.

He recently advanced to Lord St. Germain, Cosmic Christ of the Violet Flame. He is in charge of this present 2000 year cycle.

Mother Christos - The Essence of Christ Jesus blended and Embodied with the Essence of Divine Mother Mary. She is also the Dove of Peace and the Feminine Christ.

Mother Mary - The earthly name of Our Lady, as the Virgin Mother of the Holy Christ Child. She Ascended at the close of that embodiment. As an Ascended Being, Our Lady has become "Mother of Us All". She has appeared throughout the world and personally loves, nurtures and communes with many of Her children. This book is Her Gift, as is the precious *Blessed Ascension Rosary*.

Our Lady of All Nations - Mary, Queen of Peace first came to Mary-Ma McChrist under this new title on Easter, 2000. Lord Jesus had asked that Mary-Ma build a new garden for His Mother, to be called *Our Lady of All Nations World Peace Garden*. Mother Mary wishes Peace Gardens and children's gardens to be created across our planet.

Our Lady Virgin of Kauai - The presence, name, and painting given to Mary Clarice McChrist in March, 1993, when visiting Kauai, Hawaii. This image was a previous Embodiment of Our Lady, who was sacrificed as a virgin to a volcano eons ago. Her Essence has merged with all nature. Our Lady, Virgin of Kauai, also instructed Mary-Ma to prepare a grotto for the worship of the Virgin, but this grotto is no longer open to the public.

Quan Yin (Kwan Yin) - Goddess of Mercy, former Chohan of the Violet Ray. She is part of the Trinity of the Cosmic Mother. It is said Quan Yin was born from the Tears of Chenrezig, Lord of Compassion. A Quan Yin Miracle was reported in January, 2001, near Seoul, South Korea. Flowers that only bloom every 3,000 years appeared on the forehead of a statue of Goddess Quan Yin. The Buddhist monks there believe that this denotes the Sage King of the Future has come to Earth.

Sananda - A name which refers to any Christed being. For example, this could be an Arcturian Christ, but not Jesus who walked on our planet. According to Our Lord, Sananda is neither Jesus' Higher Self nor the Cosmic Christ, but one of the 12 Christs on the Inner Planes. Call upon the Name of "Jesus" as this gives Him permission to aid you and the Earth.

Shekinah - The Feminine Principle which surrounds the Father. An actual Energy Feld of the Holy Soul (Feminine Nature of the Holy Spirit) which can be seen and felt by visionaries. Also considered the feminine counterpart of Metatron.

Supreme Mother - The highest God which includes all other Gods, Goddesses, and Pantheons. She is the ultimate Tree of Life and is practically unknown to the inhabitants of Earth.

Supreme Mother

by Lord El Morya

Supreme Mother is Mother of the Twelve Sectors of Creation. Earth is in the Fourth Sector, which is everything we see in the night sky. Visualize an orange divided into twelve sections. Each section contains vast creations and Gods and Goddesses which oversee their own areas of jurisdiction.

Supreme Mother also contains 12 x 12 or 144 other metaphoric oranges which were birthed from Her Being. This is to remain a Mystery at this time. Yet Creation extends beyond all of these parameters. No being in form can conceive of the vastness of this Creation.

Glossary of Terms

Amen, Ah-Woman, Ah-Child, All One - Mother Mary's prayer closing, denoting the equality of all beings, regardless of gender or age.

Apparition - The actual appearance of Heavenly Beings, such as Mother Mary or Lord Jesus, as seen on this Earth or captured on film. (Apparition photographs are available. See Visionary Altar Art at back of book (p. 243) or on-line at: www.mothermatrix.org.

Ascended Masters - The saints and sages of all religions; those earthly beings who followed the Christ Path, perfected themselves, overcame this world, and ascended into the Heavens as did Jesus, the Christ. They work from Inner Levels (five through eleven) to awaken and enlighten humanity.

Ascension - Overcoming the Earth and the ego-self, thus becoming a "Christed Master." Originally, Ascension meant leaving Earth, with or without raising the body as Christ did. Now, it means perfecting the self, raising one's vibratory rate to that of the sixth dimension and beyond while remaining in body to serve during the healing of Earth.

The Blessed Ascension Rosary assists in one's personal ascension as well as in uplifting Earth into the higher dimensional vibration.

Avatar - An incarnation of God, either Father or Mother, Son or Daughter, who comes to the Earth as a World Teacher. This one expresses a specific divine quality or qualities of the Godhead/Godheart for a particular age. Examples of Avatars include: Lord Krishna, Lord Buddha, Lord Jesus, Lord Mary, Ramakrishna, Holy Mother Sri Sarada Devi, Sweet Mother, Sri Auribindo, and many more, known and unknown.

Blessed Ascension Rosary - Precious Gift of the Mother to Her children. Mother Mary gave this prayer to Mary Clarice McChrist in 1976.

The first stanza is the traditional Rosary as given by Saint Dominic. *Lord Mary calls this new Rosary "the most important prayer to awaken humanity and transform it during the great Tribulation."* **She requests the daily recitation of the Rosary and explains that She and Her angels gather the energy of the words, healing and transforming worldwide problems.**

Blue Rose World Service Groups - Lord Mary, Queen of Peace, has called upon you to form prayer groups across the planet. The giving of these prayers directly affects World Peace and our collective ascension. (For more details, visit the web site: **www.mother-matrix.org**.)

Bodhisattva Vow - In Buddhism, the disciple vows to stay on this Earth until all beings are Enlightened. You may have taken this Vow in an earlier embodiment. A variation on this Vow is to stay until all beings are wholly ascended and free.

Central Soul and Spirit -If you are Central Soul and Spirit of a Being, you hold the "Parental" or "Primary Essence "of that Being. If you feel you were a specific person in a past life, ask if you are Parental or an aspect or fragment of the Main Essence.

Central Sun Matrix - The Spiritual Sun/God whose Indwelling Presence is Alpha-Omega, Mother-Father. "I Am Alpha and Omega, the beginning and the end, the first and the last" (Rev. 22:13). From this Divine Source did all creation in this sector spring forth.

Christ Matrix - Is a Dispensation given after you are God-Realized. Call Lord Jesus. (3x) He will embody the Golden Christ Matrix "the body not made with hands" within your being. This is a great Mystery (see pages 36, 46, & 184-185).

Chohan - An Ascended Master who is in charge of a particular Divine Ray/color/quality of God's Light.

Cities of Light - The twelve (plus one) primary Cities of Light shall be completely lowered into the fifth dimension from the seventh dimensional fields of the Earth by 2005.

These cities are presently hovering on the etheric levels. There may continue to be changes in these details due to Earth changes or other unforeseen events. Key individuals are already being magnetized into these areas to anchor the Light. (For more information on these cities see pages 130-131.)

Cosmic Eight - An infinity symbol, an energy path connecting the levels of the self: (1) the human form, (2) the silver cord, (3) the Christ-Self, (4) the Divine Mother, and (5) the God Presence - I AM THAT I AM. (See Chart, page 40.)

Council of Light - or New Light Councils is the new name of the Spiritual Hierarchy, formerly known as The Great White Brotherhood. Mother God has reorganized the old hierarchical form of administration into Councils of Light. Council of Light may also be used to define one's personal team of etheric Master Teachers, guides, angels, and Elohim. *(A Spiritual Evaluation* given by Mother Mary-Ma gives you the names of each member of your Council of Light, your spiritual gifts, etc. See more about these Spiritual Evaluations on page 241 or on the *Mother Matrix Web Site:* www.mother-matrix.org.)

decrees - Formal prayers consisting of: (1) a preamble calling in Heavenly Beings, (2) the request set into a rhythmic pattern, and (3) a closing or sealing action. "Thou shalt also decree a thing and it shall be established unto thee and the light shall shine upon thy way." (Job 22:28)

Diamond Key - The Key to your personal ascension is earned through the daily repetition of *The Blessed Ascension Rosary*. Other specifics on this Key will be released in 2003.

Diamond Matrix - The perfect and divine geometrical blueprint of the Order of Man.

finger muscle testing - The process of getting a "yes" or "no" from your body by linking the thumb and forefingers of both hands together, which forms a chain-like connection.

Ask your Higher Self, Teachers, or Guide(s) to set up this process with you. If an answer is "yes," your fingers, with firm pressure exerted, will still remain closed. If the answer is "no," the fingers will separate by themselves.

Try it. Ask your name, age, questions you know the answer to. This is a helpful tool to verify your intuition.

God-Realization - The awesome experience of knowing the Self as God. You are forever changed from a human to a Divine Being. No one can take this from you.

Golden Age - The New Heaven and the New Earth of Peace and Brotherhood promised in Revelations 21:1. Minor Golden Ages occurred in Greece and again in the Renaissance, when humanity transcended the Dark Ages, allowing the flowering of great masters of art, music, and science to emerge. Today, humanity is called upon to shift from materialism into the spiritual destiny of "becoming the Collective Christed One".

gunas - Universal qualities: harmony, agitation, and inertia.

Helios and Vesta - The conscious Father-Mother Presence (Logos) of our physical sun. *All ancient cultures honored the Sun (Son) as an outward reflection of the Divine Source.*

Immaculate Concept - Your perfect image held by Mother Lord Mary and Lord Mary Buddha. They ask that you learn to hold your own Immaculate Blueprint or Divine Matrix, as worthy children of a loving Mother-Father God.

kayas - Time frames: past, present, and future.

lila - The Divine Play in the world of illusion.

Mandalas of Light - Energy patterns created by the recitation of *The Blessed Ascension Rosary* or another prayer or mantras.

maya - The illusions of daily life based on misunderstanding the True Nature of God and our relationship to That.

messenger - A being appointed by God, Jesus, Mary, or other Heavenly Beings, who is trained to receive and transmit an Ascended Master's Essence (energy field) and words to humanity. "If there be a messenger with him, an interpreter, one among a thousand, to show unto man his uprightness: then he is gracious unto him, and saith...'I have found a ransom'" (Job 33: 23-24). In contrast, a channel receives and transmits only the words.

Mother Matrix - Created by Lord Mary through Mary Clarice McChrist to bring forth the Mother's Word, teachings, and spiritual paintings to bless and heal humanity. On the physical level, the Mother Matrix is located where Mary-Ma resides. On the Inner Planes, the Mother Matrix encompasses all Divine Mothers, both in Spirit and flesh. It also refers to the invisible grid of the Divine Mother which moves in, around and through the Christ Grid.

overshadowed - An Ascended Master may oversoul or energetically come over a being, thus serving as a Higher Self or Teacher Energy.

Piscean Age - The 2000 year cycle in which Lord Jesus was the principle Way-Shower. We are presently shifting into the Aquarian Age when Saint Germain will preside.

Raspberry Sherbet Light - Color of the Divine Feminine, especially Mother Mary and Lord Mary Buddha. Lady Buddha introduced this color in 1991 through Mary Clarice McChrist in Mount Shasta, CA. Raspberry is a joyful higher frequency which is very useful in this dispensation.

Rays of God - The Rainbow Rays were projected out from Source. Each color has a specific meaning and represents particular divine qualities. The traditional Rays are: (1) Blue, Divine Will; (2) Yellow, Wisdom; (3) Pink, Divine Love; (4) White, Purity and Discipline; (5) Green, Art, Music, and Science; (6) Ruby and Gold, Devotion; and (7) Violet, Ceremonial Magic, Alchemy, Transmutation, and Forgiveness. Specific Ascended Masters and Archangels are connected with each Ray.

Resurrection - One of the Initiations of Christ Jesus. Resurrection is a step each spiritual disciple will eventually take. You are renewed and may be regenerated, actually becoming younger than your physical years.

Shekinah Pillar of Light - An etheric Pillar of Light representing the Mother Principle.

Solar Body - The highest individual light body on the 3rd level of the Higher Self (Monadic Level). It is also called the Sohar Body of Light (see *The Keys to the Golden Age*).

Spiritual Hierarchy - The Great White Brotherhood, composed of the Ascended Saints and Sages of all religions of the heart. It oversees humanity and is dedicated to the upliftment and progress of Earth and her children. In this new cycle, it is being restructured into Councils of Light.

Stillness - The Center Point, that which is God/Goddess within all things.

Sun of Even Pressure - The center of the Earth is symbolically the Fiery Heart Presence of Beloved Mother Earth. The Double Dorje (see page 135) is also anchored etherically within the crystal core of the Earth.

Time of Tribulation - Worldwide prophecy (Biblical, Native American, words of the Holy Mother, etc.) has warned people of impending earthquakes, floods, famine, etc. for thousands of years. **Mary says that some prophecy can be changed through praying,** *The Blessed Ascension Rosary*, **loving our neighbor as ourselves, and through selfless service to humanity.**

Vesica Piscis - Two interlocking circles which overlap. This symbol is found on the cover of Chalice Well in Glastonbury, England. This symbol is sacred to the Goddess. The rose garden in Our Lady of All Nations Peace Garden in Dunsmuir, CA also carries this symbol. It is a representation of the beginning of Creation, the initial development of the Flower of Life. (For more information see *The Ancient Secret of the Flower of Life,* by Drunvalo Melchizedek.)

Violet Flame of Mercy and Transmutation - The Blue of the Father and the Pink of the Mother combined into an etheric Light Energy which requalifies and clears negativity. Information on its use was released to humanity in the 1930's by Ascended Master Saint Germain from the Inner Retreats of the Ascended Hosts of Light. See particularly the books of Godfré Ray King: *Unveiled Mysteries, The Magic Presence,* and other teachings of the St. Germain Foundation.

The Mother Matrix Web Site:

www.mother-matrix.org

Come visit the Mother in cyberspace. Stay abreast of Mother Mary's latest messages, prayers, and the activities of the Mother Matrix. Enjoy viewing photos of Our Lady of All Nations Peace Garden. See samples of Mary McChrist's lovely visionary art. Purchase Giclée art (exact prints on canvas) or photographic reproductions and cards. Order *The Blessed Mother's Blue Rose of the Healing Heart* and other books, tapes, and CDs on-line.

Mother Mary invites you to explore *The Blue Rose World Service Groups* and find a location closest to your home. Send in your personal testimonies and experiences with the Mother.

Check out the material which features the Goddess Quan Yin. There are countless web pages awaiting your exploration. Your reactions and comments are appreciated.

Love and Blessings,
Mary Clarice McChrist

• 241

Spiritual Evaluation for You
Discover Your

**Light Ancestry - Level - Origin:
Devic? Elohim? Angel?
What type of Angel? Your Rays
Your % of Spiritual Gifts
The names of your Spirit Teachers
Guides and Primary Guide
Your Angel Helpers, Your Initiations
You will also receive a Personal Message**

Your evaluation is verified by
the Council of Light of Mary-Ma:
Mother Mary, Lord Mary Buddha,
Goddess Quan Yin, Archangel Michael,
Jesus, the Cosmic Christ & Saint Padre Pio

Love offering is $99 to $155 (sliding scale)

Other countries add $10 for priority shipping.
For a phone or personal appointment call:

Mary Clarice McChrist at (866) 223-0597 (toll free)
or call (530) 235-4117

Please send or e-mail a photo of yourself with payment.
Your five page written report and phone conference will follow.
Your photo(s) will be returned.

International orders receive a report and cassette tape.

Send checks in U. S. funds to **Mary McChrist**
P. O. Box 1178, Mount Shasta, CA 96067
E-mail: mary-ma@mother-matrix.org
Web Site: www.mother-matrix.org

The Blessed Mother's Blue Rose of the Healing Heart

with Optional CD

Mother Mary flows through Mary Clarice's voice in this CD. Mother has permeated it with Her Divine Essence. Our Lady recommends that this CD be used for daily individual or group prayer practice. A beautiful day of Grace is created when you begin your day with this CD and your prayers.

All the prayers are found in this volume. For your convenience, the page number is given before each prayer.

You may be unaware of the Power of the Word. Creation occurs with sound. The Great Councils of Light and the Ascended Masters emphasize the use of sound in chanting, mantra, and prayer.

Decrees are alchemical creations which consist of: the preamble, the body, and the closing. Decrees such as *Lord Michael,* on page 70, have a specific rhythm. They are delivered at a more rapid pace than normal prayers. Remember that the momentum of energy is gathered up by the angels. It is multiplied and delivered to the specific location where it is most required. Assistance may only be given when you, in form, call it forward.

Please share the blessing of this CD.

See the Order Form on page 243 for details.

The Mother Matrix Order Form

Name _____
Address_____
City _____ State_____Zip_____
Phone - Home_____
Fax _____ Bus._____
E-Mail _____ Web Site_____

Make checks/money orders payable in U. S. funds to: **Mary McChrist,
P. O. Box 1178, Mt. Shasta, CA 96067. Call toll free: (866) 223-0597.
International orders** call: (530) 235-4117. **E-mail:** mary-ma@mother-matrix.org

* *

I wish to order the following: Quantity Price   Total

The Blessed Mother's Blue Rose   _____$19.95*_____
of the Healing Heart* & CD**   _____$29.95**_____
  Uplifting prayers and the Blessed   CD _____$16.95_____
  Ascension Rosary to bless, heal and
  protect you and the world.

The Keys to the Golden Age   _____$19.95_____
  A precise volume which presents
  Twelve Keys to the New Millennium.
  Expected publication, Spring 2003.

The Blessed Mother's Pink Rose   _____$19.95_____
of Sanctifying Love Relationships
  Mother Mary offers practical suggestions
  and prayers to heal and strengthen relationships
  between parents, couples, and children.
  Expected publication, Fall 2003.   Subtotal_____

Priority Mail: S & H 1 book, add $6.00   Shipping _____
Book Rate: (1-3 Weeks) 1 book, add $3.00
Additional books, add $1.00 each.
Call for Quanity discounts, S & H.
Bookstore Orders: 45% off, call for S & H.
Wholesale inquiries and orders over $100,
please call. **Rates subject to change.**   CA Sales Tax 7.25% _____
International Orders or Canadian Orders: Total Due_____
please write or e-mail.

YOUR ORDERS ARE GRATEFULLY RECEIVED.
They help further the Mother Matrix and the Mission of Lord Mary.

Visionary Altar Art
by Mary Sylvia Clarice McChrist

Custom Photographic Art Reproductions. Quantity Price Total

Item	Price
The Black Madonna (10 1/4 X 15 1/4) on p. 106	$33.00
*The Lord Mary Triptych (10 1/4 X 15 1/4) (C) on p. 18	$33.00
*The Madonna & Child of Mt. Shasta (10 1/4 X 15 1/4) (C)	$33.00
*Mary of the Diamond Heart (11X14) (C) on p. 32	$33.00
*Archangel Chamuel/Babaji (10 7/8 X 18) (C)	$33.00
I Serve the Grail (11 X 14) (C) on p.166	$33.00
*The Grail Lady (10 1/4 X 15 1/4) (C)	$33.00
*Chenrezig, Lord of Compassion (10X15) (C)	$33.00
*Mother of Protection (10 1/4 X 15 1/4) (C)	$33.00
*Lord Mary Buddha (10 1/4 X 15 1/4) (C)	$33.00
* White Buffalo Calf Woman (10 1/4 X 15 1/4) (C)	$33.00
*Also available as a Visionary Card	$3.00
Add one mailing tube @ $6.00 for 1-4 large photographs.	$6.00

Custom Giclée Prints on Canvas also available. Call for prices.

Visionary Art Cards

Color Reproductions, blank inside, with prayer on back.

Item	Price
*Mother Mary of the Diamond Heart, on p. 32	$3.00
*Lord Mary Buddha, on p. 111	$3.00
*The Madonna and Child of Mt. Shasta	$3.00
*Chenrezig - Lord of Compassion	$3.00

* Also available as cards. 1 to 7 cards shipped Priority Mail Flat Rate @ $3.85.

Marian Apparition Photosgraphs (5"x7")

The Black Madonna/Mary Magdalene, on p. 108	$6.00
Italian Mary, on p. 90	$6.00
Mary's Face (Medjugorje, Yugoslavia)	$6.00
Madonna and Child (Medjugorje)	$6.00
Invisible Mary (Medjugorje)	$6.00
Mary with Rosary (Scottsdale, AZ) on p. 79	$6.00
Jesus Shroud of Turin Photograph Touched by Sai Baba	$6.00

Subtotal _____
1 to 7 cards or photos shipped Priority Mail Flat Rate @ $3.85. Shipping _____
California residents add 7.25 % Tax_____
Total due_____

Shipping: Canadian Orders are 1.5 times above rates. For International orders, add an additional $10 for Priority Shipping. Rates are subject to change.
Make checks or money orders payable to: <u>Mary McChrist</u>.
P. O. Box 1178, Mt. Shasta, CA 96067
Call toll free: (866) 223-0597 or (530) 235-4117
Web Site: www.mother-matrix.org   E-mail: mary-ma@mother-matrix.org